Nyla Ditson

Blinded

ISBN: 978-1-312-98469-1

Other Books by Nyla Ditson

Titles available on Amazon and Lulu books website, in eBook and paperback formats.

Angelic- A Christian fantasy novel about guardian angels and suicide not being the answer but God.

Miracle Monday- Based on the true story of how a book was given to someone to save their life the night they planned to commit suicide.

My Boaz, His Ruth- A fiction godly relationship advice book about a girl whose best friend is told by God who the girl will marry.

Someone to Hold- A Christian romance story of falling in love with someone who later becomes famous.

Dedication:

For anyone who has ever experienced a bad body image day. I've been there countless times myself and I pray this story's message is as comforting to you as it is to me!

Scriptures:

Proverbs 31:30

"Charm is deceptive and beauty is *fleeting*, but a woman who lives in awe of Christ is to be forever admired."

Luke 4:18

"The spirit of the Lord is upon me. He has equipped me to provide for the needs of the poor, restore sight to the blind and heal the broken and crushed."

Prologue

They say love is blind. I don't know who *they* are, but I know they're right. That three word phrase isn't just a fairy tale thought but a truth statement, evident in our realities. I learned the accuracy of that small sentence the summer I turned twenty one. Through *seeing* life through the eyes of another. The eyes of his heart. He used his unique circumstance and ability to love to change me. Change the way I viewed myself and others in the world. How I viewed beauty and the meaningful in this short life. Love is an ability, a power that we all possess. Whether we choose to use it for good or neglect the gift is up to us. My name is Cara Phelps. This is my story. How love taught me to view myself as beautiful, the way I am today.

I'll take you back to the beginning of that summer. We met at the end of June. I'd been working in the city of Saskatoon the start of summer but then took my uncle up on his offer to work at his restaurant. Packing my black four door Dodge up, I waved goodbye to my roommate and headed west, driving past vivid green and gold farming fields, ending up in the small prairie town of Kindersley, Saskatchewan…

Chapter 1

"Hello?" I call out, letting myself in, my duffle bag dropping to the kitchen floor.

Footsteps followed by a crash. "Ouch!"

"Randy! Get your foot out of my face!"

"It's not like I intended to put it there, Jill!"

I stifle a laugh. There are no two people quite like my aunt and uncle. "Are you guys alright?" I move towards the sound of the crash, into the computer room. After rounding the hallway corner, I gasp as the sage green walls come into view. More specifically, I gasp at the scene between the four walls. "What happened?" I take in the sight of them, mouth agape.

Uncle Randy grunts. "Oh, didn't you know? We decided to take up yoga."

One eyebrow raises and my eyes widen at the sight of the broken lamp on the floor, next to their twisted monkey piled bodies. I reach to help my aunt to her feet. "You've certainly got the pretzel look nailed."

She brushes her jeans off, casting a glare at my uncle. "*Someone* thought I was too short to reach the lamp to change the light bulb and *insisted* on helping. Before I knew it, his hands were reaching above me to grab it the same time I am. Naturally, I let go since there is no sense in us both lifting it from the book shelf." Aunt Jill's bright blue eyes hold a look of frustration but also patience learned from thirty plus years of marriage to the 6'1, bald man in our midst. "But then we both let go at the same time!"

Uncle Randy pulls himself to his feet. "And everything went kaboom!" He glances down, speaking to the inanimate object in our midst. "I never much cared for you," he tells the lamp, peering at the various pieces scattered on the carpet. "It's actually a blessing you're naturally deceased. Now I don't have to think of a plan to kill you."

"Randy! You told me you loved that lamp." Aunt Jill's hands fly to her slim hips. Only five foot three, and a quarter she always reminds me, but a feisty woman. "You even bartered the price down at the garage sale for me."

Uncle Randy winks at me. "And that, my beautiful niece, is the secret of a happy marriage."

I laugh. "Lying?"

He shakes his head, our family's trade mark blue eyes sparkling. "Putting your loved ones wants above your own." He wrinkles his nose, once again looking at the crime scene on the carpet. "Even if it means bringing the world's ugliest lamp home to live with you for ten years."

"At least it wasn't twenty," I supply, leaning in to his hockey jersey covered chest, accepting his welcome home hug.

"Yes, however would I have survived another ten years of torture?" Uncle Randy slings an arm around me. "Glad to have you here, kiddo!"

Aunt Jill watches us, a smile on her smile. "Cara, it's been far too long. Randy, move your arms out of my way so I can hug the girl!"

"Nah, group hugs are better."

Aunt Jill rolls her eyes but I see her smile. She's wraps her arms around us. "Oh, it's going to be so nice to have a fuller house for a few months."

I nod, pulling away. "Where's Jack?" I can barely wait to run my hands through his mop of blond curls, so similar to mine. As the youngest, I sometimes wished for little siblings. But little cousins, like nine year old Jack, are God's answer to that desire.

"At a friend's." Aunt Jill nods to the doorway and we follow her out in to the spacious kitchen. "Let's get you set up downstairs. The room at the bottom of the stairs is all yours."

I know where it is. I grab my bag. "Okay, thanks."

"Need help with your bags?"

"I'm good. Thanks anyways, Uncle Randy."

Twenty minutes later, I've moved all my things downstairs, located the plug in for my phone charger and texted my mom to tell her I arrived safely. Now I'm seated at the kitchen island, trying not to drool as my aunt whips up a batch of her famous chocolate chip banana muffins. "Mmm," I inhale deeply, closing my eyes. "I can't remember the last time I had homemade baking."

"Who did this?"

My eyes flip open. Uncle Randy's standing beside the island, frowning.

"Who I ask you? Who?" The frown deepens.

I can't tell whether he's upset or joking. You can't really be sure when a middle aged man is holding an opened package of double roll toilet paper. "Is there something wrong with that brand?" I glance at my aunt, drying her hands on a chequered towel. She leans against the sink, looking equally as confused. Well, maybe slightly less. She *has* lived with Uncle Randy's sense of humur much longer then I have.

Suddenly, Uncle Randy's tree trunk arms wrap around the plastic package. "Not at all!" He gazes lovingly down at the toilet paper. "It's the best thing to happen to man since satellite TV. We can't ever go back to a different brand, Jill. There is simply no comparison."

My mouth gapes. So does Aunt Jill's. We look at each other. Then at Uncle Randy.

"What?" He gives us a funny look. "You're both crazy for not being as passionate about three ply as me." "It's a valid family discussion to bring up."

Aunt Jill's palm smacks into her forehead. "God, you sure gave me a strange man to love."

"Ah, but you love me, woman." Uncle Randy smiles at his wife. "But seriously, don't buy anything else. This stuff triumphs." Like a kid with a bag full of candy, he grabs a sports magazine from the countertop and retreats to the bathroom, whistling as he goes.

Again I look to my aunt. She runs a hand through her short curly brown hair, identical to mine in length and texture except in color. "That man keeps me young."

"I think Uncle Randy is hilarious. Strange is just a synonym for personality. Conversations are never boring with him."

"Between him and Jack there is never a dull moment in this household. Sometimes I wonder if there are hidden cameras in here and I'm actually a character on a sitcom."

"I wouldn't be surprised if you discover a camera while dusting one day." I'm just about to offer to help her cut up vegetables for salad for supper when the front door opens. "Cara!"

"Jack!" I jump down from my bar stool. "Hey, buddy!" My arms wrap around him tightly. "How was your friend's house?"

"Awesome! His mom made us cookies." Jack pauses to sniff the air. "And my chocolate senses detect a presence of more in this room."

I laugh alongside Aunt Jill. *Ah, it's going to be a good summer living with this lovable bunch. God, thanks for blessing me with these people as my family.*

And within a day, I would meet another who would soon be a part of my prayers of thanksgiving. Someone who would divide my life into two categories. Life before Joey and life after.

***

After a delicious supper of baked salmon, alfredo pasta and salad, Jack and I walk down to get a movie. Yes, Netflix's and rentals right from the TV are available but I've always loved the quality time and conversations on the walk to Walmart to search through the pile of five dollar movies. From the looks of Jack's eager eyes and how he keeps bouncing as he walks, I'm not the only one enjoying the fifteen minute walk.

"What's new, buddy? Haven't seen you since the family reunion last summer."

"I've got a girlfriend."

"Oooohh!"

"She's going into grade four."

"Whoa! An older woman."

A shrug. "What can I say? I'm an attractive catch." His expression turns thoughtful. "Like salmon. That was good tonight."

I ruffle his wild bond hair and he ducks out of my touch. "I love hanging out with you, Jack."

"You're fun, too."

"Excited for school to be done next week?" I cringe, finding myself asking the cliché questions that arise during certain seasons. I remember having to give my standard answer each time an adult asked me.

But Joey doesn't look bothered. "Do zebras have stripes? Is the sky blue? Does Jesus love you and me?" He grins, cheekily and I echo the look, loving that he and I got put into the same family.

"Point taken, little cousin."

And so our conversation to Walmart goes. No lulls whatsoever and lots of laughter. We walk through the automatic doors side by side, the air conditioning a welcome relief from the summer heat. It's almost seven-thirty pm but the heat is still as relentless as it had been mid-afternoon. We make our way over to the bins in the back by the electronics section. "Let's try to get something everyone will enjoy." I toss a cartoon DVD aside and dig deeper, feeling like I'm searching for a specific grain of sand on the beach.

"How about this one?"

I glance over at the cover Jack's holding up. It's a title I remember watching a few years ago and not being impressed by it. "It's not that great." We search silently for a minute. "How about this one?" I ask, smirking, holding one up.

Jack looks up from reading the back of a cover. Curiously, he takes the DVD from me. I enjoy watching his expression change to shock. "No way! I am not watching *Strawberry Shortcake*."

"You sure? I think you'd like her."

He grins and sticks out his tongue. "And I found a *Dora the Explorer* DVD a few seconds ago. Don't even think about suggesting that gross girl stuff."

About twenty minutes later, we agree up on a Disney movie neither of us has seen yet. On the way back, we pass by a park and decide to stop for a while.

"You know what I don't get?" Jack asks me as I spin him on the merry go round. "Old people."

I give him another push. "What's not to get?"

"They remind me of raisins. I don't want to look like a dried fruit." He sticks out his foot, dragging it through the sand, slowing the merry go round. Jumping off, he walks to the main playground center. I follow him up the stairs and then sit down next to him on the double person slide. We don't even have to ask if it's a race. We've visited this park together too many times in the past. We have established cousin routines.

Jack looks over at me, a gleam in his eye. "One..."

"Two..."

"Three!" we say in unison and push off.

It's a tie.

"I wonder what I'm going to look like when I'm old," Jack asks on the walk back.

"White hair and wrinkles, most likely."

"My mom has wrinkles."

I snort. "Maybe don't mention that to her."

"How come?"

"Some people don't like their wrinkles."

"Why?"

How to explain the concept of body image and poor self-esteem to a nine year old? "People get very caught up in their outside appearance, since it's the first thing people get to see." Sensing an opportunity for a life lesson, I continue. "But it's what the inside looks like that's more important." Jack nods at my words but to me, they feel like piercing arrows. *What a hypocrite, Cara. Trying to tell him something you have such a hard time believing yourself.* I shake off the negative voice. Now was not the time to give into those thoughts. "Do you know what another name for wrinkles is?"

Jack kicks a pebble with his shoe. "What?"

"Laugh lines."

Ironically, wrinkles appear on his usually smooth features. "Seriously?"

I notice that's his newest favourite word to respond to a statement. He likely picked it up from school. Jack must have said it at least half a dozen time on this walk. "They call it laugh lines because some wrinkles are caused by laughing. And laughing is so good for us in life." I poke him playfully in the side. "It feels as good as eating those chocolate banana muffins of your mom's!"

He giggles and pokes me back. "I like the sound of your laugh, Cara."

"Thanks. Wanna race back?"

He grins, that lovable cheeky one of his and then takes off, sprinting across the green school yard. I follow close behind, letting him win.

Laughing and out of breath, we sling our arms around each other and walk into the house. Jack hops up on a bar stool and I help myself to some water from the tap. I've just taken a sip when I hear him ask his mom a question. "Mom? You need to laugh more. Maybe I'll get you a joke book for your birthday."

She looks up from an open cookbook on the island. "I do laugh, Jack."

"Your wrinkle count says differently."

"You have been spending too much time with your father. I have no idea what you're talking about."

I am no help in explaining. All I can do is spit out my water and try not to choke. I'm laughing so hard it hurts. But oh, it feels good.

***

There is no such thing as skinny enough. Or pretty enough.

"There is no win in comparison," is how well known Pastor Andy Stanley once said. Either you feel guilty for feeling better then someone or bad about yourself for not measuring up. It's fine to gain inspiration or motivation from others, but comparing? Nothing good can come from it.

But it doesn't keep me from doing it.

Sighing, I step out of the shower. If only I could say recovery from an eating disorder has completely freed me from believing lies about beauty. If only I could say I'm finally content with the body I'm in. If only...

A knock on the bathroom door. "Cara? Mom wants to know if you'll be ready in time to leave with us."

Water still dripping off my shoulders, I wrap a fluffy towel around myself. "No, you guys leave without me," I reach for a second towel to wrap my hair in. "I'll take my car and meet you at church."

"Okay. We'll save you a seat! Service starts at ten-thirty. Don't be late! Last one there is a rotten egg." I picture Jack scrunching up his face into an adorable frown. "I wonder why they say that. It's not like you stink when you're late."

"It's just an expression, Jack." I hear him make a thoughtful sound before his loud footsteps take off down the hall.

I open the closet and reach for my brush. Aunt Jill cleared a shelf for me to put my toiletries in. Until the downstairs bathroom's new shower is installed next week, I'm sharing the upstairs one with the rest of the family.

My eyes flicker to the ground, to the white digital scale. *Don't do it.* I hear the voice of caution whisper. *With your past, you know it's not a healthy thing.*

The number of the scale is a warped thing, once dictating my emotions. I led myself to believe for so long that the lower the number, the better I would feel. Yet, I distinctly remember how I felt two years ago, staring down at a scale that read ninety four pounds: miserable. I was starving myself through high school and early university years. And what was gained by my enormous loss? Happiness? Attractiveness? Admiration? No, at the end of the day, it all came down to me clutching a grumbling and aching stomach in order to ward of the intense hunger. Just as I clung to my stomach until sleep would fitfully come, I hung onto the lies that it was worth it. Beauty would be worth the pain.

Skin still pink from the hot shower, I rub the fogged mirror with my fist. Another sigh. *Why does being healthy have to be so hard?* I turn to the side, judging my body from the new angle. I can truthfully say I've recovered from being anorexia but these extra thirty pounds, healthy or not, are still a struggle to love. To accept.

"Curves are just a synonym for fat" is a hard voice to silence some days. It's something I'd told myself for many years, instilling it as truth. It's still a fresh and vulnerable to break new habit to see curves as an indication of a healthy and vibrant woman. As my counsellor put it, curves and healthy body weight are indications of truly living. These things were results of a full, well rounded life. She said balanced life should be celebrated.

I try to have real life woman as role models, not celebrities on magazine covers battling eating disorders themselves. As a rule, I don't buy those magazines anymore. They just make me feel bad about myself. Instead, I look up to people like my sister, cousins, my counsellor and other woman in my life.

My eyes run over my towel clad body, taking in my curved out backside and my chest. My no longer toothpick

17

arms. Still a flat stomach but definitely not rail thin or resembling the body of a twelve year old boy.

"Curves," I mutter to myself, knowing it's time to step away from the mirror. "Signs that I'm making healthy choices. Eating healthy amounts and enjoying fresh and nourishing foods. Being active. Resting and enjoying good company and laughter." That's near perfect wording to a truth statement my counselor told me during my last session, six months ago. She advised me to talk back to the negative self-comments in constructive ways.

Easier said than done, especially on "fat" days like today. I know the mirror and photographs can say one thing but my feelings can dictate an entirely different thing. I glance at my gold watch on the counter. Ten after ten.

I ready for church quickly, hating the rush but glad for the refreshing feel of the shower. Putting on my pearl studs, I stand back and survey my look. Blond wildly curly grown out bob hairstyle. Natural amount of makeup. Sprinkling of freckles across the bridge of my tanned nose. White blouse. Red beaded necklace. Heels. Black high wasted skirt.

"You look... beautiful?" The word comes out as a question. Even after months of practicing positive affirmation to attack the negative, it still feels wrong, almost sour on my tongue, when directed at myself. Not every day, but on large breakfast days, light workout days or just random days. After defining beauty as rail thin for so long, it will be a while for me to undo the mental damage. One day, I hope I can consistently see a healthy body as beautiful.

The second sigh of the morning signals it's time to go. I'm already late. And like any other insecure day, I catch myself wondering if the time spent judging my body and worrying has been worth anything. Or rather, a meaningless pursuit that distracts from more important things. Like using the body God has given me to lead a full, content, giving and satisfying life. The kind of life that allows for me to undistractedly love God with all my passions, muscle and might. The end of that paraphrased Bible verse also mentions loving others like you love yourself.

But what if I don't love myself? is an unanswered question that follows me all the way to my car.

***

I slide into the fourth pew from the front, next to my aunt. According to my watch, I'm exactly twenty three minutes late.

Aunt Jill raises a dark eyebrow, smiling.

"Sorry," I mouth, slipping off my black blazer. Why I thought I'd need an extra layer in this heat is beyond me.

Jack makes a goofy face, filling his cheeks with air and tugging at the bottom of his ear lobes. I mimic the look, getting an elbow from my aunt but a delighted giggle from my cousin.

Uncle Randy, sitting between Aunt Jill and Jack, is too wrapped up in the Pastor Harvey's announcement to even notice my arrival

"Next week, our church is on to supply volunteers to help with the school days held, at Luseland Bible Camp." The slim, sharply dressed, white haired pastor glances down at his notes. I vaguely recognize him from previous summers. I think there's a picture of him and Uncle Randy wearing polo shirts and holding golf clubs, in a frame somewhere back at the house. "Schools spend the day at the camp as their summer field trip. Though we can't talk about spiritual things, we can love on the children with our actions. By making them feel loved and helping be a part of a fun day, many kids end up signing up for a full week of Bible camp later in the summer..."

I tune Pastor Harvey out. Usually church announcements, the worship songs and the sermon hold my attention. Crowds, especially church since it feels like a safe haven, keep me blessedly distracted from my self-esteem battles. They help me take a step back from the insecurities as I survey a bigger picture and purpose for life. But today it isn't a crowd serving as a distraction.

It's a him.

A rather good looking him. I sit up straighter, craning my neck to get a better view of the boy sitting diagonally from me, two pews up.

"And now I'd like to call up my son, Joey Waterloo, for special music." The Pastor Harvey gestures to someone. "He'll be treating us once again to an original piece."

To my surprise, the boy I'd been admiring stands.

My eyes widen. *He has to be 6'3, at least.* I'm 5'6 myself and don't normally feel small. *But I bet I would next to him.* I watch him move from the end of the pew to the piano. He takes his time, walking slowly, eyes forward. With a creek, he sits down on the old wooden bench, strangely accompanying a sleek looking black grand piano.

Adjusting the microphone, he opens up with a few words. "Good morning! What a wonderfully sunny day! God is good!"

That is a lot of exclamations for one very small sentence. "All the time," I respond back to the familiar saying, alongside the rest of the congregation.

"And all the time?" Joey asks, his face lit up.

"God is good!"

"Amen to that!" Joey laughs, looking at his father, now seated on a stool to the side of the pulpit. "You always hog that line, Dad. I had to try it out just this once. I see it's still a crowd pleaser." I swear, even from this distance, his eyes are sparkling. They look twice as blue as mine and people often remark how bright mine are. The "Sapphire Eyes" is what my family refers to the common eye color in our relatives.

As the congregation smiles, some chucking, clearly familiar with Joey's enthusiasm, I narrow my eyes. Who is this boy? Curiosity washes over me, like buckets of drenching water. Sometimes you meet someone and you instantly just want to be a part of their life, to be their friend, to get inside their head. To know their passions, their dreams and desires. What they are like on an early Monday morning or how they would describe a perfect Saturday.

All I know right now is typical information gleaned from first impressions. Tall, dark hair, and lanky yet athletic build. Plain but tasteful grey dress pants and a black long sleeve dress shirt. I noticed on his walk to the stage, his white and black Converse shoes. *A hint of his personality peeking through,* I think with a smile.

Joey didn't take any sheet music with him. "So this is a new one, guys. It's called 'What's Left of Me''. Softly, he begins to play the intro, creating a pretty background to his explanation of the songs message. "This song speaks truth to the lies we often believe. That we aren't good enough, a failure, unwanted, unimportant, weak or unbeautiful."

My heart skips a beat.

"Those lies are seeded by the king of lies," Joey shakes his head, passion for the topic ringing in his deep voice. "Satan loves using trickery to deceive us." The background music grows, more noticeable but still soft enough to hear him. "There is only one way to drown out those lies. Not by human will power, but by *God* power. Next time you hear a lie calling you a false name, imagine what God would say in response to that voice."

With a deep breath, Joey dives into his song. It's the most inspiring song I'd ever heard. His fingers skillfully fly over the black and white keys. A glorious combination of euphoric chords, flats, sharps, fortes and crescendos fill the air. The music sounds like that of angelic beings, a choir of heavenly hosts.

But his voice is even more stunning then the music. A combination of jazzy Michael Buble's voice and Jason Mraz's earthy soulful sound. "So keep on judging, through your crooked eyes. Keep on telling me I'm not worth anything." Joey's singing voice is even deeper than his speaking one. "I'm done listening to all the hate and the lies. I've found hope beyond compare at the foot of the cross."

The chorus is my favorite part. I'm not sure what I enjoy more. The beauty in the lyrics or watching Joey sway to the music, eyes closed, swept up in the moment. Not once does he look down at the placement of his fingers. "So here I am, down on my knees. Broken and surrendering, what's left of me. It's all Yours, Lord." By the end of the song, I have the chorus memorized, having heard Joey repeat it multiple times.

When the music ends with a final chord, applause breaks out around me. Clapping alongside them, my eyes follow Joey all the way back to this seat. I don't recall what his father's sermon is on that day. All I remember is staring at the back of a certain someone's head, silently singing to myself the lyrics of "What's Left of Me".

God clearly wanted me here this Sunday, to hear those words. *Am I judging myself through crooked eyes?* I wondered throughout the sermon. *Is it a lie when I see myself fat and weak for gaining weight because I'm heavier than the miserable anorexia me?*

No audible voice answers. Neither God nor my own conscious. Yet, I know the truth. Of course it is a lie. But just because your head knows it's a lie doesn't force your heart to believe it.

I want to talk to Joey afterwards, shake his hand and thank him for sharing his song. But the greeting line at the door where he stands shaking hands next to his dad is long. And Aunt Jill has a ham cooking in the slow cooker and Jack is "So hungry I could eat about six and a half horses."

So I slip out the church front door with the rest of the family. I look Joey's way, hoping to catch his eyes and share a smile. But he's looking down, laughing with a kindergarten aged child. It's bright out standing in the sun. His gold aviator sunglasses cover up his eyes.

Maybe another day I'll get to see if those Pacific Ocean blue eyes are actually the shade they seem...

Chapter 2

Monday morning is my first day at work. Waitressing has its pros and cons. You get some customers who make you want to morph your customer service smile into a snarl. But it's a guarantee you'll eventually get a table you can have fun with, joke with and actually enjoy serving them throughout their stay. Thankfully, my last table of my shift is the latter. Waitressing my way through university has led to many end of shifts with me close to tears. Exhaustion from walking between the kitchen and tables all shift, combined with cruel people who take their bad days out on the next person they come into contact with, can be lethal. One time, I had to get my co-worker to do my final cash out for me. I was too upset to sort the receipts in my apron into various credit card transitions or to figure out my tips earned from my cash float. But like I said, not all days end like that.

I'm working the opening shift, still being trained for the first week, from seven in the morning to three in the afternoon. Lunch was hectic. My uncle's restaurant, The East Side Café, is a local hot spot, newly renovated and located very close to a main highway. From breakfast specials to Greek salads, their famous mushroom cream soup, taco salad bowls and cheesecake desserts, the menu is both small but loved by locals and the oil field workers passing through.

As a waitress, you never know if you'll get to sit down for a meal. Usually, you know you won't be able to eat at a "normal" food break time. I ate some cereal and fruit early in the morning before work and then scarfed down a protein bar around two in the afternoon. It sure made me savour the unrushed supper meal at five-thirty with the rest of the family.

After a short nap afterwards, I join Jack on the couch. He is watching *The Big Bang Theory*.

We watch in silence, only adding to it with our laughter. Sometimes it's just nice to have company after a long day.

"Where did I put it?" Aunt Jill walks into the room, looking under a throw pillow on the brown leather chair.

"What are you looking for, Mom?" Jack asks, his eyes never wavering from the TV screen.

"My phone." Hands on hips, she looks around the room in disbelief. "The last time I remember having it was at church. I pulled it out to check the time mid-service. But I'm sure I put it back into my purse."

I stretch my hands above my head. "Did you call to see if you left it there?"

"It's on vibrate."

"No, I mean, did you call the church office and see if it had been turned in?"

"No."

"Mom?" We both turn to look at Jack, squirming in his seat, looking uncomfortable. "I might have done something bad."

Aunt Jill narrows her eyes. "Jack, what did you do?"

He licks his lips, nervous. "After church, I was so hungry but you guys where still busy talking." His ball cap smashed down over his wild curls comes off, a hand distraction to play with. "So I took your phone out to play a game on it and I think I left it on the pew instead of putting it back." Mouth pinched and shoulders slouched, he looks about to cry.

Aunt Jill crouches in front of him on the hardwood floor. "Aww, honey. Thank you for being honest with me. But you need to ask for permission before you use things that don't belong to you."

Jack hangs his head, refusing eye contact. "I know. I am a bad kid."

She pulls him in to a hug. "Not at all. Just a human one." She releases him from the hug and ruffles his hair. "What do I always tell you about mistakes?"

"Use the lesson learned from them to make better choices the next time."

"You got it." Aunt Jill looks up at me. "Cara? I hate to ask but I need to run to the grocery store before it closes. Would you mind driving to the church to see if my phone is there?"

"Sure. You coming, Jack?" Uncle Randy is still at the restaurant, discussing the last of some kitchen renovations with the rest of the management team.

Jack clicks off the TV. "I think I'll go with Mom. She keeps buying gross cereal. I need to sneak in some sugary stuff."

I laugh. "Sounds like a plan to me." I lean in close to whisper. "I suggest hiding it under the Bran Buds in the cart."

He covers his mouth, trying but failing to muffle his voice. "Broccoli would make a great decoy, too."

From the front door, I hear my aunt laugh followed by the front closet opening. "I can hear you two!"

Jack and I exchange grins. "Mission abort?" I ask him.

He shakes his head, eyes mischievous. "Never." Placing a hand on his chest, he puffs it out. "No mission is too impossible when Frosted Flakes or Fruit Loops are on the line."

I follow him to the door and watch him grab his superman wind jacket. The temperature hasn't dropped but the cool breeze makes it a bit chilly today. "Sounds like something you and your dad would discuss."

A final look before he follows his mom to the car. "Because we did. Yesterday at breakfast. Dad said he didn't know if he could make it."

"Make it?"

"Make it through life eating Raisin Bran one more day."

I grab my car keys and follow him out. I'm still smiling when I pull into the paved church parking lot seven minutes later. Killing the engine, I step outside. I walk up to the doorway, stuffing my sunglasses in one pocket of my sweater and pull the heavy door open.

Good thing it's open. I didn't even think of that. My eyes slowly adjust to the dark as I make my way to the auditorium. *Strange. It's open but no lights on.* I walk by a mirror on my way.

I stop.

I can't help it.

At work, I'm so busy rushing around, trying to remember where I put my order notepad and trying to remember the daily specials. The long mirrors in the restroom mirror make my body look lean, complimented by the mandatory black clothes. I don't have time to be insecure about my new healthy body. Not for very long at least. But here, in this moment, time is all mine.

I tilt my head. After work I changed into a blue and white speckled bunny hug with white tassels. Flip flops and dark wash capri jeans complete the laid back look. Smelling of greasy fries, sweat and having sticky pop soaked through my black dress pants demanded a shower post work. My hair air-dried during supper, even curlier then before, thanks to the humidity today.

It's not like supper was unhealthy. Aunt Jill always includes a salad and the BBQ chicken was a lean protein choice. I resist the urge to lean in closer and evaluate my cheeks which suddenly seem too full, my jaw line not as sharp and defined as it once had been. *Maybe it's because I didn't do a workout today? But my job includes physical activity.* With a strength not of my own, I literally feel God's arms gently guiding me from my negative thoughts and evaluations. From my cries for help, He and I both know its unpredictable how I feel about my body. Some days, like after a tough workout, I feel strong and powerful, thankful for my body. Or on days spent with family that remind me of the important things in life. But today, a fresh new transition for the summer in progress, it's hard. My routines are different and I'm resorting to the familiar. *Maybe it would be best if I avoided mirrors all together.*

God, protect me from myself. Help me not to go back down any foolish roads, I pray urgently, feeling a wave of anxiety rising in my throat. I don't want to start restricting food again in order to feel good. Or to begin over exercising again. I'd already learned from discussions with my counsellor and past experiences on my own that those things don't lead to happiness. They might make me feel powerful and accomplished and strong willed for a while, but then weakness inevitably comes.

Not enough fuel for a body to perform isn't fun. It plays with your mind and energy levels. *And that is not an image of happiness. Cara, stop comparing yourself to the old you. She wasn't happy or healthy. She was wasting away. Remember what Uncle Randy told you yesterday evening?* He'd been watering the flower pots outside after supper and I'd tagged along, walking through the backyard with him. He'd been quizzing me on the ideal elementary school I'd want to work at, once I earned my Bachelors of Education degree through the University of Saskatchewan.

"Cara? Can I tell you something?" he'd asked when there was a lull in the conversation, dipping the green watering can. A stream of water flowed inside a pot filled with white pansies.

"Sure."

He finished watering the pot and then set the can down. Arms crossed, he stared down at me, looming over me with his height. "You look good, healthy."

My heart and head didn't know what to feel or think about that.

He noticed my struggle and pulled me into a hug. "Your eyes look more alive now, honey. And I'm not afraid of breaking you when I hug you anymore." The hug lasted a full minute before he pulled back, arms still on my shoulders and searched my watering eyes. "You look beautiful, Cara. I hope you feel it."

The memory dissolves. Why is being called healthy so hard? It's what I wanted. And it is true. I do feel better physically. I have more energy to spend with family. I'm not forced to head to bed early for lack of energy. I also have energy and motivation to spend on hobbies and friends. And I can now share bonding time over meals with others. I'm more balanced now, incorporating healthy amounts of food and exercise into my everyday life, including interactions with people in those things.

 Just a bad habit to break, defining beauty like culture does. I step into the dim auditorium, trying to shake the insecurities from my mind like a dog shakes water from his fur.

Music fills my ears. I realize I'm not alone.

Illuminated by a small piano light, sits a young man at the piano on the stage.

Joey.

The song is one I recognize. "Mighty to Save", a song we sang at church yesterday. I slowly make my way up to the stage, not sure if I should interrupt. I don't want the glorious music to end but I'm eager to speak to the pianist himself.

In the end, I wait until the end, savouring the sound as I close my eyes, standing by the edge of the front pew. "You are very talented," I say when he's finishes. "Your song on Sunday was breathtaking."

Joey jumps. "Oh, thanks." He holds a hand to his heart. "I thought I was the only one here." He looks in my direction, oddly wearing sunglasses indoors. "I don't recognize your voice. I'm Joey Waterloo." A mischievous grin, similar to the familiar one Jack wears. "And who should I refer to as the woman responsible for my near early death, due to heart attack?"

Laughing, I extend my hand to him to take. "Cara Phelps." Strangely he doesn't take it. So I let my hand fall to my side, confused.

"Phelps, as in a relative to Randy and Jill?"

"Yes." *That's odd that he didn't want to shake hands. His face and voice are still friendly and seem open to this conversation.*

"Randy is my dad's golfing buddy."

"I hate golf."

Joey grins. "You have to admit, it's more entertaining to watch then curling."

I match his wide smile, feeling my eyes dance. "Very true."

"So Jack's your," Joey pauses, searching for the right family relation, "cousin?"

"Yup. He's quite the entertainer, even at nine."

Joey chuckles. "I love that kid. During the school year, I teach him piano lessons once a week. I'm sure going to miss him. Next week is our last session."

"Been playing long?"

"Since I was five."

"I notice you don't use sheet music."

He gives me an odd look. "No, I haven't in a while. I play by ear and memory now." When I don't respond, Joey hold outs his hand. "Nice to meet you, Cara."

"Likewise." I take it feeling relieved, figuring he didn't see my extended hand before in the dim lighting. Approval of others is something I really crave. Rejection is just about the cruelest feeling for me. "I meant what I said, your original piece on Sunday was moving."

"Got a lie that needs exposing? Like the song talked about?"

I give him a funny look.

He pats the seat beside him. "We all do. Nothing to be ashamed of. Tell me about it and I'll tell you about the one I struggle with."

I hesitate. I've never met someone so direct, so intent on digging into the deep corners of my heart and life so quickly upon introduction.

"Seriously, I mean it. I was sitting here playing and praying that God would cross my path with people to build into their lives and have them do the same for me. Praying for people to encourage and be encourage by." He tilts his head in my direction. "Pretty sure you walking through that door is a very quickly answered prayer. So shoot." He leans back, crossing his arms over his deep grey v neck t- shirt and waits. I glance at him, his plaid shorts, his flip flop still positioned on the pedal, at the glowing exit side on the other side of the room, then back at him.

I sit down.

It's dim in the auditorium. I still can't see his eyes. "Why do you wear your sunglasses inside?" I finally ask, breaking the silence, not wanting to open up to a stranger about my struggles. But I want to get a glimpse of who Joey Waterloo is.

"Oh, right." He removes them. "I forgot to take them off."

How do you forget to take off sunglasses in a dim room? It hits me, slamming into my chest and stealing my breath in surprise, the second I get my desire to meet his eyes. Yes, they are as blue as I imaged. Like the blue of the cloudless June sky outside.

But they are also the eyes of the blind.

"I see, I mean, you don't see…" Blood rushes to my cheeks. "I don't know what's wrong with me." Abruptly, I stand. "I should go."

"Can't be friends with the blind?"

I smack my seat back down. "No, I don't care about that. Makes no difference." I struggle for words. "When I make a fool of myself through words, I don't tend to make it a habit to stick around."

He's looking at me, but slightly focused to the side of where my face is. "Hey, don't worry about it. It's not like I force those around me to eliminate the words, *seeing* or *eye* from their vocabulary." He laughs, the sound echoing through the empty room. "I'm the one that jokes, to the groaning of my friend and family, that it's my dream to meet my future wife on a *blind* date."

I snort back a laugh. I like this guy. So open about his faith. So direct. So funny. Laid back.

"Want to go for a walk?" Joey stands, reaching to close the piano top.

"Uh, sure."

He whistles. "Mac!"

Expecting another male to appear, I'm surprised to see a golden retriever come bounding down the center aisle, tongue hanging happily out of his mouth. He reaches Joey and nudges his leg, announcing his arrival.

Joey reaches down to scratch behind his ear. "Hey, Mac. Meet the cause of my near death, Cara Phelps." He lowers his voice to a whisper. "She's related to people I can vouch for though. So don't worry, I'm pretty sure she's not an axe murderer."

Trying to hold back laugher, I fail miserably and take the paw Mac adorably extends and shake it. "Pleasure's all mine, Mac."

He barks happily.

I lift my eyes to Joey. He's looking at me but again, not directly. I have a feeling in time I will get used to it. Like the movie I recently saw, *The Fault in Our Stars*, where a girl had a respiratory disease and needed to wear an oxygen tube in her nose. Half way through the movie, I barely noticed it any more, too caught up in the storyline and the personalities of the characters. "Is he a seeing eye dog?"

"Yes, I've had him for two years." Joey searches for something on top of the piano. I'm about to offer help but then realize he'd been doing fine before I came here and might be offended by the offer. I've always looked at people with disabilities as in need of an abled body to help them. But after spending only minutes with Joey, his personality so confident, I sense this boy is no different than I. Maybe he has to modify things and go about them differently, maybe taking more time to do them, but he still deserves the dignity of being independent and respected. Just like anyone else with a disability. Not to be called a blind person but a person first, who happens to also be blind.

Finding what he was searching for, a leash, Joey whistles for Mac. He clips on the leash to the red color around the dog's golden fur. "Ready for a walk, buddy? With a beautiful girl?" He looks at me. "And I haven't seen my reflection in a mirror for four years, probably forgot to comb my hair today. Hope you and Mac won't be embarrassed by being with me." He stands, letting Mac lead. "But God is good. Since it's so windy, your hair will soon be as equally as similar to Einstein's as mine."

"My hair's normally pretty wild, even on a calm day. Curls run in the family gene pool."

He pauses, waiting. "That's your cue," he whispers. "What I said at the start of that sentence."

"All the time."

"And all the time?"

"God is good."

"Man, I love that line! I can't wait until I'm done Seminary and get to use it every Sunday."

"You're in seminary?"

"Online classes." We walk outside. "There is some awesome equipment for the visually impaired out there. I listen to all my classes on audio and for typing, I have a special software that allows me to speak into a microphone. Then my computer translates it into written format for my professors to evaluate. No more cramping hand from holding a pencil after taking notes. Hallelujah!" He pauses for a quick breath, his eyes lighting up with excitement. "For now, I'm the music pastor at church. Technically, you don't even need to go to seminary to be a pastor but I want to. It has been really beneficial so far. I love leading the music portion of things but one day, I want to speak. I've given the sermon on the occasional Sunday but I crave to do it more. Originally, I started university to be an engineer but couldn't finish for personal reasons. But this is definitely more up my alley, anyways."

I'm thoughtful, letting his dream declaration settle in. His explanation is long but fascinating. I'm loving getting a window into this boy's world. I so very badly want to ask him to explain what he meant by personal reasons. The thought that he wasn't born blind suddenly flashes to my mind. I shove it away, scolding myself for even thinking I could ask someone something so personal, so soon. "You said I was beautiful." I finally say. "But you can't see me."

"Ah, but I can."

"Liar.

We leave the parking lot and step onto the side walk. Mac leads the way, sniffing the ground. He seems to know where we are going. Perhaps it's a familiar route for the pair. "I can clearly see parts of you that others can't," Joey tells me confidently.

"What do you mean?" We reach the opening of a walking path. Mac gives a small bark.

"You got it, boy, go in, "Joey nods to Mac. To me, he explains. "The pavement changed. I can feel it. We walk this forty minute loop a lot in the summer. When your sight is gone, you start to be more sensitive to other things, like the differences in grounding. That's how I know where we are."

"Hmm," I match his leisurely pace, enjoying the scenery of bushes, trees and wild flowers surrounding the manmade lake to the left of the trail. "So you were saying?"

"Right. It's the same thing with the people. I can't see people's physical features so I am more in tune, at least more quickly than the average person, to what their inner appearance is. Their words and tones become more significant to me, since it's all I have to get a feel for them during a first impression." He casts a quick glance at me, golden aviators back in place. "You seem rather beautiful to me, Cara."

Heat rushes to my cheeks and I look away, forgetting he can't see me. "How could you possibly know that from one conversation?"

He stops walking abruptly and turns to face me. "I'm being completely honest with you. I sense it in the way you greeted my dog, the way your voice lit up with affection when we were talking about Jack and in the way you got flustered when you thought you offended me when you found out I can't see." He's looking directly at me this time, right into my widening eyes, almost as if he isn't blind. "You're a beautiful soul, Cara. Even if you don't accept that fact yourself."

We start walking again and I'm quiet. How can Joey know so much about me?

"It's a gift" he replies, as if reading my mind. "God sometimes gives me a sense about people. And I get a sense that's the lie you are struggling with, seeing yourself as you actually are."

My jaw drops.

"Sorry, kind of deep for our first conversation." Mac barks as two young teenage girls approach on rollerblades. Joey takes the cue to step to the left side after Mac pulls lightly on the leash. "Let's talk about something else," he offers once the girls have passed.

Thankful for the change in topic, I ask "Why is his name Mac?"

"It's not because I love Big Macs, if that's what you're thinking." I laugh. Between Joey, my uncle and Jack, I'll definitely have my laughter quota for the day. "But I am rather fond of Macintosh toffee," Joey confesses. "Braces for two years were torture."

"Let me guess, the day they were off you ate yourself sick of it?"

"Pretty much." Joey presses a button on his silver watch. A robotic sounding woman's voice tells us the time is eight- forty-five.

"Why do you wear sunglasses?" I've been trying to be considerate of the questions I ask but this one has been bothering me.

Joey swats at a mosquito near his face. "Though I'm considered legally blind, I can still sense some light, especially when it's particularly bright." Mac barks to announce a couple walking hand in hand, approaching us on the path. Joey greets them at just the right time, likely waiting for their footsteps to signal their distance from us. Even being around him for twenty minutes is opening my eyes to a foreign world of the sightless. How they accomplished what they do and modifications to do what others do unconsciously. When their footsteps fade behind us, Joey continues. "To some people, it's useful for sensing object locations through light reflections." He shakes his head, running a hand through his dark straight but mused hair. "Not me. I find it's more of an annoyance then anything. It's distracting when I'm playing the piano or when I'm trying to have a conversation with someone." He nudges me in the shoulder, walking closer. I think it's on purpose. "Plus, before the accident, I always thought I looked like a rock star in my aviators. I figure losing my sight doesn't have to change that."

My laughter fills the breeze as we round a corner, a slight hill coming up.

"Aren't you going to ask?"

"I am kind of curious. It doesn't bother you to talk about it?" I truly do want to hear about how he became blind.

"Not all." One glance into his open blue eyes and I know it's true. "The accident happened four years ago...." I listen to his story, the only sound I contribute for the next twenty minutes is my flip flops hitting the ground. It was a university basketball game, during a final. Joey had gotten a break away and been running in to score an easy layup to tie the game.

Slipping on untied laces hadn't been on the agenda.

One minute he was the source of the crowds cheering, ecstatic on their feet and the next he was the cause of a collective gasp. He can't recall the next moments since the second the back of his head smacked the gym floor, he blacked out. His only recollection of it comes from his parents and friends accounts.

"They called the ambulance, rushed me to the hospital and strapped me to a board. The next few days I was in induced coma as they ran multiple tests on me. They knew I'd be terrified when I woke up and the tests on my brain required I be completely still."

My heart hurt for him. "What was it like, waking up?" I ask, quietly, unsure if it is too personal to ask.

His answer is slow, though he's probably been asked it multiple times. "Like a nightmare." Mac tugs on the leash in Joey's hand and he takes it as a cue. "There's a bench overlooking a scenic part of the lake. Mac and I usually stop here for a breather. It's a good spot to think."

I sit down next to him on the wooden bench, carved out of tree trunk. Joey's right, the view is surreal. Bushes outline a slight slop leading down to small sandy shore. There's the hint of the arrival of sunset glimmering in the water before us. Evergreen trees and shrubbery create a private talking spot, slightly off the main trail.

He doesn't continue on his explanation on waking up blind. I let my imagination fill in the blanks. If it were me in that nightmare, I bet it wouldn't be a pleasant memory to be asked about repeatedly. *I can't blame him for not elaborating. Especially to a stranger.*

"Hey," I nudge his knee with my own. "Thank you for sharing your story."

He keeps his gaze on the water, looking but not really seeing. "I'm used to it. Sometimes it's easier to tell and then other times..," he sighs and I know it's one of those times.

I don't usually open up to people so quickly, so personally. Joey's personality seems like he does, that I'm not the only one who's heard this version early on in a friendship. But there's something about him, a certain quality that makes me believe he genuinely cares about people and their own stories. That he cares about their hurts and wants to help them. It's an attribute that will one day make him a great pastor, by compassionately visiting sick members of his flock who are in the hospital or by encouraging people struggling with personal matters.

People like me.

"You're so joyful and friendly," I comment, remembering his enthusiasm at church, his humor this evening, and his ease of living with a disability.

A sad chuckle as he reaches to pet Mac. "I wasn't always this way. I wouldn't have blamed my parents for disowning me, they put up with a lot of attitude. After the accident, I was even on some depression meds."

"Friends and family are supposed to love at all times," I answer, remembering a verse I've memorized from Proverbs. "And it's during those hard times, that people need support and a friend the most."

He gives me a sideways look, again eerily appearing to maintain correct eye contact. It's almost like he again has a heightened sense that I'm in a situation myself right now requiring a friend. "Yeah," he finally agrees. "But I was not a nice person to be around."

"You were dealing with a lot."

"It doesn't give me the excuse to take out my misery on others." He stretches his hands over his head, his t-shirt coming up slightly to revel a flat stomach. "But my dad helped snapped me out of that."

"What'd he do?" I picture the passionate pastor from Sunday. Clearly, Joey got his passionate nature from his Y chromosome.

Hands return to his side and then Joey shrugs. "We had a hard yet helpful heart to heart. He shared some scripture with me, of people who had suffered far greater things then I was. How their attitudes where still positive and their lives left a legacy, despite living with obstacles."

"Like who?"

His answer is slow, his eyes blinking once, twice. "Jesus," he finally says softly. "He was mocked, beaten, betrayed by his closest friends, and murdered in an excruciatingly painful way. But He did so willingly, enduring pain even for those who caused Him such suffering and pain. In the process, Jesus left a legacy of love behind Him."

Moved by his answer, I gaze out at the water, envisioning scenes of the crucifixion I'd seen in Mel Gibson's *The Passion of the Christ*.

"Want to hear my story?" I surprise us both by asking. Even Mac's ears perk from where he lays at Joey's feet. Though I'm sure it has more to do with a robin that landed near the bench then my question.

Joey angles his body toward me, arm around the back of the bench. "Only if you are comfortable sharing."

Suddenly, I'm not feeling so open, despite having gotten a glimpse in to Joey's vulnerable heart. "Could we plan to meet up later? It's kind of a long story."

"For sure." Joey stands and I follow suit. We get back on the walking trail. "Want to watch a movie on the weekend?"

I smile. "I'd like that." It appears I'm not the only one enjoying a stranger's company tonight.

By the time we reach the end of the loop, back at the opening to the trail, my face hurts from laughing. Innocent eyes but purely playful at heart, Joey's been entertaining me with the advantages and disadvantages of being blind.

"Who wouldn't want a friend they can pick their nose freely *anytime* and *anywhere* in front of?" He teases. "Who knows, you might have been digging for boogers all night and I never would know it."

I nudge him. "I have not!"

"I'll never know for sure." We reach the church parking lot. It's nearly dusk and I suddenly remember I forget to look for Aunt Jill's phone.

"I just realized my family is probably wondering where I am." I explain why I was at the church and we head inside. The phone is right where Jack said it would be. I pick it up and toss it from one hand to the next. I don't really want this night to end but it's inevitable. After apologizing for taking up his evening, to which he shakes his head and thanks me for *wonderfully* taking up his time, he explains he was just practicing since he's on worship team next Sunday. Joey assures me that he has all week to practice. I ask him about being on the worship team. Eventually, I run out of things to stall with and offer a simple and drawn out, "So..."

My reason for procrastination is completely see through. I get an adorable grin. "So..."

"Got any more funny advantages?" I ask, pulling at anything I can to prolong the moment.

Joey strokes his chin thoughtfully and it makes me wonder what he would look like with a five o'clock shadow. *I bet ruggedly handsome.*

"My mom's glares of disapproval are pretty much ineffective now."

I laugh. "Nice. You still live at home?"

He squats to the floor, untying Mac's leash form his collar. "For now, it's easier. I've lived there my whole life," he explains. "I know the layout, the number of stairs, what each room has for potentially hazardous furniture. It takes some effort to 'learn the room' of new places." He gestures around him, indicating the auditorium we are in. "Dad's been the head pastor here for fifteen years so I knew this place with my eyes closed, even before the accident."

"That must have been helpful."

"Very much so. As was the year of schooling I took in California." Leaving Mac to chew on a toy in the corner, we move towards the front door and into the cooling evening air. "They taught me braille and how to use alternative techniques and equipment to function in normal life in a typically sighted person world."

"I've never heard of such a school."

He leans again the closed front door. "Changed my life." He face breaks into a lazy grin, a look I'm starting to become pleasurably familiar with. "It's where I discovered I didn't have to give up my love of rubric cubes. Turns out, they make speciality ones, using braille lettering to indicate what each colored square is."

"You will have to show me that sometime."

"I will, at our movie date on Saturday."

I shift my weight to my right leg. "So, it's a date?"

Joey lowers his sunglasses suggestively and wiggles his eyebrows up and down. "Oh yeah. Just try to resist me." After we both laugh, he continues. "In all seriousness, I like you, Cara. I'm glad we crossed paths tonight."

If my sweaty palms and racing heart and lurching stomach are any indication, he doesn't know the half of it. "The feeling's mutual. Thanks for the walk and chat."

"Thanks for listening. Today was kind of discouraging school-wise, with marks and stuff. I think we both needed a friend tonight."

"Totally a God thing we crossed paths," I know he agrees even before I see him nod.

A friend of Joey Waterloo. I liked the sound of that. I don't ask about the day, he would've elaborated if he wanted. Even after an evening together, I already know he isn't one to need prying in order to share his heart.

After exchanging phone numbers and addresses, I wave good bye and head for my car. *A date,* I think happily, pulling the seatbelt belt over my shoulder. I'm still not sure what he was implying completely. Despite his words, I still feel we are still pretty much just acquaintances, but on borderline friendship. *And who knows what that could turn into?* I turn on my driving lights and lift my hand to wave at Joey, still leaning against the church.

Seeing his glasses, I remember and drop my hand. Sadness for the wonderful boy living in a dark world fills me. *No more star gazing, sunsets, seeing loved one's faces.* But just as soon as the thought comes, another takes it place. *But at least he can still play the piano and hear his beloved music.*

I steal a look in the review mirror as I leave the parking lot. Joey's heading back inside, hearing my car tires growing distant. *What a nice guy,* I think all the way home. *There is a reason I'm here this summer*. I break into a replication of Joey's lazy grin. *And I'm thinking it might have something to do with one beautiful boy, with a heart as open as the night sky and laughter as easy as a child's.*

Yup, this summer is going to be golden.

Chapter 3

"How was work?"

It's Friday night, an impromptu movie night at Joey's house. I've been looking forward to it all day at work. I thought our plans for a Saturday movie night would be the next time I'd get to see him.

"Fine," I lie, sitting down next to him on his front step. Mac lifts his head to look at me from the bottom step. I stroke his fur, enjoying the softness. A breeze blows through my curls and gently sways the yellow and purple pansies in the flower garden in front of us.

Joey stretches his long legs out, interlacing his fingers to crack them. I cringe, choosing not to tell him my opinion on that particular habit. "What's it like to be a waitress?" he asks. "Do you like it better then lifeguarding?"

At least I don't have to wear a swim suit and constantly be around other woman with bikini worthy bodies. We've been texting throughout the week and I mentioned working at a wave pool in Saskatoon for the last few summers. "I think I like serving better, even if it's busier work. Especially during popular meal times." I stretch my legs out, copying Joey's stance. We both wear dark wash jeans. "Some days I wake up already tried just thinking about moving around all day, trying not to spill drinks, remembering who ordered what and recalling what ingredients are in our daily specials."

"Ever spill anything?"

A hint of a smile, even though the memory's unpleasant. "Once I dumped a whole jug of ice water on an old man. He used to be a regular but never came back after that." I visualize the incident, remembering the mortified feeling and hearing my hasty apology. "The other waitresses actually thanked me afterwards. They said they were glad I finally got rid of Mr. Walter and his bad moods."

"A hero by butter fingers." Joey's hand reaches to pet Mac, touching mine already on the retriever's fur. I move away. Sparks tingle on the spot on my hand where our skin touched. A smile teases at the edges of Joeys lips. I love his smile, it reminds me of Jack's childlike grin, appearing when Aunt Jill announces we are having ice cream sundaes for dessert. "I didn't know your hand was there. I would say sorry," Joey's gaze turns away from looking blankly at the flowers. His blue eyes have picked up golden flecks from the early summer evening sun, "but then I'd be lying."

I understand. I squirm. I feel butterflies.

And I like it.

We talk about our weeks. Joey shares some of the humorous things Jack said at his last piano lessons and we exchange our favourite parts of summer so far.

"Want to watch that movie?" Joey asks, leaning back against the navy sided house. He'll be listening, I'll be the only one watching. Apparently he still enjoys spending time with people through movies.

"What one did you have in mine?" I stand, brushing dust off the seat of my jeans. Runners, jeans and an old favourite orange t-shirt feel lovely after running around all day at work in heels and black dress clothes. I'm thankful I don't job shadow the closing shift, noon to eleven in the evening, for another week. Small town or not, Friday's are officially date night. Translation? A guaranteed hectic night shift from start to finish. Tonight I'm all for relaxing in good company.

I follow Joey inside. His parents are ironically out for a dinner date themselves. Joey and I plan on ordering in pizza. "Something with explosions, *please*. Or some other manly theme." Joey guides himself with the railing through the dozen stairs leading to the main floor from the small front entry. "I watched a chick flick on Tuesday with my sister and mom and I'm still having nightmares." He scratches a spot on his dark hair, pausing at the top of the steps to look back at me. He still tries to participate in eye contact as much as possible, just as anyone with sight would during proper times during a conversation. "Relationships do not happen like that in real life. Love within an hour and a half is ridiculous. Makes me want to vomit." He turns away and steps onto the main floor.

I follow behind him, impressed by his confidence in footing. *I guess his memory of the house would contribute to that.* "Movies show the passage of time," I argue in defense of my beloved romantic comedies. "A lot of them are set in a course of a longer time frame then what ninety minutes would allow for us to accomplish in real life."

"I suppose. But the romances still seem rushed." Joey searches for the phone. "But I guess I do know couples who have met and married within six months." He hits a few buttons on the cordless phone and grins in my direction. "Important numbers are on sped dial, pizza guy included."

I listen to him strike up a friendly conversation with an apparent acquaintance working at the pizza shop. While I wait, I look around the kitchen and notice photos covering the fridge. Intrigued, I walk over to get a closer look.

At twenty four, Joey is the oldest of two. There is a picture of him and his twenty three year old sister, Erica, sitting side by side on a piano bench, grinning at the camera, likely about to play a duet. Erica has his same rich colored dark hair but unlike Joey, deep chocolate brown eyes. Both siblings are striking but in a natural way. Joey speaks fondly of Erica, saying they are close and that it's common to be mistaken for twins. He told me over the phone, at nearly at two in the morning, that Erica was his personal encourager four years ago when he had his basketball accident.

"She got so angry at me when I would be moping around, feeling sorry for myself and angry for not stopping to tie my shoes." Joey's voice had held a fondness for her. "Erica told me I was being irrational and just plain stupid. That it's not like I'd left my shoe untied so I would purposely lose my sight. She reminded me, quite loudly, that I had just been caught up in the excitement of the game. That it was an accident, simple as that." I liked Erica's tough loving spirit, saying the hard but truthful things that needed to be heard. I hoped I'd get to meet her this summer. She was camping with her boyfriend's family this weekend. Like me, she was home from Saskatoon for the summer in-between the university school year.

It still feels odd to think I'll soon be watching a movie with a blind person. But Joey told me he enjoys listening to the stories, same as he does listening to audio books. He texted me once, saying it was a "Sweet deal having someone read to you regularly." Texting is similar as his phone has a specialized feature that reads his texts out loud. Sometime slang or misspelled words have pretty funny pronunciation but he gets the main idea of most texts.

"So, what's your story?" Joey leans back into the couch in front of a black flat screen TV and props his feet on the glass coffee table. There's a bouquet of pink and red roses in an elegant glass vase next to a set of wooden coasters.

"Nice roses," I say, joining him on the couch, not ready to share. I thought I had one more day to prepare, to muster up courage. I'm pretty sure our original movie night for tomorrow is still on. Maybe I could postpone it until then. *No. I should do it tonight. It won't get any easier with time.* I want to share, really. Just like Joey opened up to me on our walk on Monday. It's just not easy for me to share my brokenness and poor life choices to someone. The things I still struggle with. "Are the roses from your dad, for your mom?"

A sly smile reveals straight teeth, proof of Joey's braces years. My procrastination is duly noted. "They're from my mom's garden in the back." I peer at them more closely. I like them better than the typical closed petal style roses. This particular variety's petals are spread wide, with visible yellow middles.

"Hey," Joey finds my knee. "You don't have to share, if your story is too personal. We can just be friends from here, no travelling to the past required." Knowing he's being truthful, that I shouldn't feel obligated to share, I find a strength not of my own.

I suck in my breath sharply then release it slowly. *Okay, God. Help me do this, to let this boy in.* I look down at Joey's lean fingers, pianist's hands, still resting on my knee. His touch give me courage and support to be brave. "No, I want to tell you."

And then I'm off, diving head first into a sea of overwhelming emotions. It's not a place I allow visitors to see, outside of my old counsellor and my parents. I'm not proud of my past, even if it's made me stronger today from hard lessons learned. But Joey gets an invite inside my private world tonight.

"It all started in high school," I begin, drawing my knees to my chest, hugging them. Joey's hand falls to his side. "I fell prey to the lie that the smaller I was, the better my life would be. That all my problems would be solved. But under a hundred pounds felt like I'd been banished to hell." Joeys groans as I say my past weight. I'm facing the dark TV screen. Now I'm the one who's looking but not seeing my surroundings.

Floods of images fill my mind. A montage of moments. Struggles. Shuffling my papers in grade eight English to cover my grumbling stomach, a clump of hair coming out from brushing, sitting on the sidewalk during a short walk, completely exhausted, my finger trailing down the calendar weeks passed with no appearance of a period. There are others, even more painful. The agony of that helpless time assaults me, crawling at my insides. I see myself clutching my head in a fetal position as I rock back and forth, on my parents kitchen floor, devastated when I'd realized I drank my brother's 1% milk instead of my own skim milk.

I explain some of these pictures from my past to Joey. Some I keep to myself. I know it's deep and personal but Joey's expression doesn't look shocked or judgmental. Only pained for what I went through. Correction, what I *put* myself through. But this friendship's foundation is being formed on honesty, just liked he'd been with me on our walk. I don't always share this side of me with new friends but I really want Joey to know about it for some reason. "It got to the point where I worried about calories in toothpaste." I rest my chin on the top of my knees. "I even refused to eat food out of dishes I knew my family had eaten junk food in."

Joey's quiet, letting me talk.

It's not pleasant to revisit these memories but it feels good to expose the past. To know I'm telling my tale to someone who cares. "My lowest weight was ninety-four pounds," I admit, remembering how the numbers had terrified and not satisfied me. Fear had sliced through me that day on the scale in grade ten, during summer holidays at my aunt and uncle's. "The thought of continuing my misery, restriction and obsessive rules about food was exhausting, even to a properly fuelled mind and body."

"What do you mean by rules?" Joey asks, moving slightly closer.

I look over at him, debating whether to reveal more of the eccentric behaviors of the obsessed. But it's Joey, so I answer the question. "Things like not eating the same food twice in a day. Or having to eat all of one kind of food before moving onto the next kind on my plate." I think for a moment, trying to recall more." I would tell myself my mouth was closed for eating between times not typically designated as meal time. So I would only allow myself to eat from seven to nine, noon to one-thirty and five to seven. And no snacks, ever." I clutch my stomach instead of my knees, my hunger for supper now nothing compared to the many nights I willingly sent myself to bed starving. All in the name of remaining unnaturally thin. Indescribably miserable.

Joey groans again. "Cara, I can't even image living like that. I'm *so* sorry."

"Don't apologize. I did it to myself."

"What finally changed?" he asks after a moment of silence.

"I remember looking up my body mass index on a chart during a nutrition class in university." The next part is hard to share. "I was sickly happy when I discovered, in relation to my height, my weight was categorized as underweight and malnourished."

"Cara..."

I move away from him, not wanting to be touched or hugged. At least not yet. "In my eyes, I had achieved success." And culture's approval in becoming their definition of a beautiful size. Envious comments of others didn't help matters. "But I was hurting in a bad way and I knew it. I was breathing but not actually living."

Respecting my need for distance, Joey folds his arms across his green university bunny hug. "Did you tell someone?"

"Yes, my mom. It was the hardest thing I've ever had to say, admitting I had an eating disorder." I thought it was weak thing to do, that I could manage on my own. But deep down, I'd known I couldn't. "If I didn't seek professional help and the support of loved ones, I could very well still be anorexia at seventy. Still as unhappy and bound with chains as I was then." My lack of control, my box of consuming darkness with no doors or windows or way out, was killing me. Obsessive thoughts filled my days. What to eat? How much? When? How many calories were in this? How long would eating this require me to exercise to burn it off? At times I would exercise in order to burn off *all* the calories I'd consumed. Some days every time I ate, even if it wasn't an unhealthy food, even an apple, would make me feel fat. "Fat's not a feeling", my counsellor informed me. But insecurity, anxiety and low self-esteem are.

"I got into a lot of arguments at meal times with my family," I shared. Food is a way to connect and bond with people through a mutual need to be nourished. Yet, I was so consumed with what I ate that I was depriving myself of good conversation and company, too concerned with the calorie content in what they would eat. "Sometimes I would make up excuses to avoid going to restaurants or to other people's home for dinners. The lack of control in the food I would receive there was terrifying." My distorted view of happiness and my body robbed me of so much life back then." *And it still does, in a different way.* But I keep that confession to myself.

"It was a sign of strength," Joey says, breaking into my silent thoughts. "Asking for help."

"I know." Still, the memory of that painful season in my life is hard to walk down.

"Did you go to counselling?"

I nod, then remember it's only for my benefit. "Regularly, for a year and a half. I don't go anymore, though I'm glad I did. God free me, through giving my counsellor wisdom."

The doorbell rings.

I jump, tense from my tale. Joey remains motionless.

A second ring.

Rising, Joey slowly walks to the door, opens it and pays for our two pizzas. Pepperoni and Tropical Chicken. He's friendly with the delivery man but he's off. I can tell he's distracted from what I've told him.

When he returns to the living room, pizza boxes in hand, I study his pained expression. *It's like he feels my pain himself.* You can share a trial with someone, try to use words to give them a taste of it, but until they have experienced something similar, they can't truly know the depths of despair you've walked through. *But that expression reveals his sympathy. And maybe compassion is needed over empathy.* Wordlessly, Joey leaves and grabs a two liter bottle of Coke from the fridge and two glasses from the cupboard. I'm still amazed at the graceful way he moves, never bumping into anything but expertly maneuvering through the room. Sometimes he uses a hand on a wall or piece of furniture for a guide or as a reminder of where he is in the room.

Once again, Joey sits next to me. "Tell me more," he says, the first *Transformers* DVD on the coffee table forgotten for the moment.

And so I do. Throughout the next twenty minutes, I explain how Saskatoon's Christian Counselling Services changed my life. Or more specifically, how God used the one on one counselling services to transform me. I explained some of the techniques I learned and still use today to support healing and recovery from an eating disorder.

Joey makes a move for the pop. I'm torn. *Offer help or not?* I really don't want to offend him or make him feel like I'm treating him like a child.

"Don't worry," Joey says, settling the choice for me. "I know by practice how long it approximately takes to fill this size of glass." He demonstrates, filling the glass three quarters to the top with pop. "And as a rule of caution, I stop pouring a little ahead of time."

I take the glass he hands me then watch him pour another. We sip our drinks, neither one making a move to open the chequered box of pizzas on the coffee table. The bubbling cheese aroma smells amazing but our conversation still feels unfinished, requiring our full attention.

"You know," Joey sets his glass down, looking at me with those gorgeous blue eyes that any girl could easily get lost in. "As humans, we'll never be rid of our natural need to belong and be accepted." His hand covers mine. "But we *can* change the way we view ourselves."

"How?" I whisper, leaning closer to him, wanting to hear his wisdom.

"Confidence goes a long way, Cara." He takes his hand from mine and I miss the feel of it. "Like my song said on Sunday, there is freedom at the foot of the cross. From believing the lies and the hate. Use God's voice to expose the lie that you're not beautiful or don't measure up to others. Or that you're not as good as the past version of you."

He just *knows* my struggle. I hadn't said a thing about struggling with my new body. But Joey's lack of sight truly does give him sensitiveness in other areas. Tone of voice. Hidden meanings behind words.

"Sometimes it's so hard to be happy in a healthy body," I admit, though I'm sure he knows already. "And even if I don't act upon the destructive impulse that come sometimes, to restrict food or over exercise, the anxiety over my body's new shape can be equally as destructive."

"Totally understandable. Each time you tell yourself hurtful things, you've basically kicking your self-esteem to the curb."

This I know all too well. "It's a hard habit to break, to redefine a definition of beauty you believed for years." I picture myself, judging my legs in my short-shorts yesterday afternoon. I'd been disgusted with the "jelly" skin that wiggled. Rationally, I know I'm fit from regular runs, yoga classes and walks. I'm at a healthy weight now. "It's so easy to fall back into old ways of thinking. Especially since what I see in the mirror is what I once feared becoming." My voice catches, emotions I've kept squished down striking me. I've only revealed this next thought to myself and God. My throat thickens, making speech impossible. A reassuring hand to my shoulder as I lean over my knees, pained. "The old me would consider the current me... *fat*." The word "fat" comes out bitterly, like a swear a child says but knows better.

The strong hand squeezes my shoulder. "Try imaging what God would say to that lie, Cara."

"I can't." My eyes squeeze shut, the internal pain suffocating, my anxiety over a lack of control becoming a dictator to my emotions. The funny thing about an eating disorder is it appeals since it's something you can control in your life. But in the end, it controls you.

"Then I will for you." Joey pauses, probably praying for wisdom and words. "I think God would say to that lie this: 'My previous child, Cara, think of the stunning sunsets streaked with oranges and pinks. The majestic snow peaked mountains. Tropical destinations with tall palm trees and sandy beaches." I listen to Joey's words, his face in a squint, like he's listening to God telling him what to tell me. "God would remind you He is the artist of those and that your admiration of those scenes prove you think they are unquestionably beautiful."

I'm so caught up in his words. It's like I can feel the hands of God reaching out to me through Joey, pulling me from my past, from my depths of helplessness. I sit up with a jerk and search his eyes, desperate to hear more, to memorize the confidence in his words I see in his eyes.

Joey's voice grows softer but never loses its certainty. He reaches out to me, finding my face, my chin. He lifts my chin with one finger, so I have to meet his eyes. They are focused slightly away from me but I don't care. "God wants you to believe, Cara, that those wonders of the world are His creative artwork and so are you. You both share the common factor of possessing His signature in the corner of you. His beautiful works of art."

I bite my lip. *Who is this boy?* So mischievous and humorous at heart one second, then wise beyond his years in another setting.

"Pounder that truth statement, Cara. Keep using that technique of using God's response to the lies as your powerful defence."

Truth statements? A concept not unfamiliar to me. My counsellor had me write truth statement sentences on recipe cards. Bible verses about beauty fading but my inner appearance being what should be admired and praised. Written reminders that impulses and bad feelings will fade. "You sound like you've been in counselling yourself." I feel my eyes narrow, finding it hard to imagine this lanky boy beside me ever needing someone else's wisdom.

"Because I was," Joey's stomach growls and he moves his hands from my face. He take the sound of his stomach as a cue to open one of the cooling pizza boxes. "The first year after the accident. I needed help to deal with my depression." He hands me a paper plate and napkin. "I was so caught up in believing the lie that my disability would define me as weak and a burden."

He goes into a little more detail then sighs. "But I'm not like that now. God got a hold of me and made me realize I still had the gift of life. I could still make a difference in people's life and change the world. Just differently now." Another sigh. "But I'm human, prone to forget lessons learned. Sometimes I still do let doubt creep in, making me view my blindness in a negative and limiting way." He feels around and finds the box of pizza and grabs two pieces of pepperoni. "Pretty deep conversation for a first date."

Date. I *really* liked that word in association with this friendship. "Just a bit."

"Thanks, though. For opening up. It's inspiring, how God healed you."

"Thanks for listening. And not judging. Obviously, I'm not healed completely."

He gives me a side glance. "No one has it all together. We are all hurting in some way. It helps *so* much when you have Jesus though. It makes not having everything together easier knowing He does. That He's guiding your life and not you." Joey reaches for the remote. "Someone once told me a friend loves at all times and it's during the hardships that we need friends the most."

"Sounds like a pretty wise woman," I smile, remembering the night I told him that.

He pushes play and leans back as the screen come to the life, a trailer for an upcoming movie beginning. "Very. I can't wait to hear what she'll teach me next."

Feeling warm all over, I fill my plate with a slice of Tropical Chicken pizza. I pick a piece of pineapple off and stick in my mouth, chewing thoughtfully.

I cast a look to my right. Joey has his typical smile on, eyes closed as he listens. I think I have my answer now. I know who this boy is.

A Godsend.

Chapter 4

Half of me wishes we watched a comedy instead of an action movie. Our conversation left me feeling encouraged but emotionally drained. But Joey has me laughing as soon as it's over, making funny comments about the cast and crew names as the credits roll down the screen.

"*Bean* as a last name? How unfortunate. People just automatically assume you have constant gas."

Or my personal favourite of the night: "Pit?" Joey scrunched his nose, making me burst out in laughter since he looks so ridiculous. "Doesn't make me wonder if he's a relative of Brad. Just makes me glad his first name isn't Harry."

"Thanks for the evening, Joey." I say as he walks me to the door around ten.

"We should definitely do it again. Oh!" Joey snaps his fingers. "I meant to ask, would you be up for bowling tomorrow instead of another movie night? Some young adults from church are going."

I think about it for a moment, adjusting my purse strap. "Sure," I finally agree. "Sounds fun."

"They're an awesome group. You'll love them."

And that's how I spend my weekend, bowling with five other twenty something aged young adults. Like usual, Joey has the group holding their stomachs in pain from laughing. The muscles in my face get a good workout that night. They're still sore Sunday morning.

Watching Joey at the piano in his suit and tie during church is rather enjoyable. Afterwards, I join him and two others I met at bowling for lunch at Subway.

"You've never blown a bubble?" An outspoken girl with long blond dreadlocks, named Mandy, asks when the topic of the best gum for bubble blowing comes up. She snags a Sunchip from the orange chip bag in front of her boyfriend, David, a quiet Asian. His style is very preppy and sophistication, dressed in a striped green and white name brand polo and khakis.

"No." Though I'm not exactly sure why. "I think maybe I was scared of getting gum in my hair and having to cut it out," is what I finally conclude after a moment's pause.

Across from me, Joey sets his take out cup of iced tea down with slam, similar to a judge adjourning a court. "This tragedy must end today!"

"Yeah!" Mandy's green eyes light up. "Anyone have gum? Let's teach Cara right now."

Before I can protest, pockets and purses are emptied. A collection of various brands of gum are thrown into the center of the table.

"Any Hubba Buba?" Joey asks, rolling the wrapping of his finished sub into a tight ball.

"Sure is," Mandy hands a white wrapped square piece to Joey. "She's all yours."

Oh, does that sound good. "Is Joey the bubble blowing king?" I ask, a little confused.

Joey blows at his nails and shrugs, trying to look humorously modest. "Yours truly is the current record holder for most gum used in a bubble."

David speaks up, for the third time in total the entire course of lunch. "Twenty six pieces of Hubba Bubba, wasn't it?"

"Twenty-eight." Joey corrects then winces and rubs his jaw. "I paid the price for that dare for a few days." His blue eyes turn to my direction. "How shall we do this?" Fingers snap, a mannerism I'm learning to associate with inspiration. "I know!"

Mandy and David exchange smiles. They've known Joey longer than me. I'm sure their imaginations of what ideas Joey can come up with are more creative than mine.

"Let's pretend you're an alien who's just touched down to earth," Joey says slowly, the idea still forming itself as he speaks, "who's never experienced gum before. And we," a gesture around our four seater table in the corner of the fast food restaurant, "are the humans who get to break down the steps of bubble blowing to you."

I laugh. "You are so weird."

An unoffended shrug. "A compliment, really. I'd be insulted if you thought otherwise. Weird just means personality to me."

I shake my head. *God, you sure got creative with this one.* "Okay, fine." I lean forward in my seat, Joey's enthusiasm for life contagious. "Let's do this."

Joey holds up the *Star Trek* greeting that accompanies the words "live long and prosper" with his fingers. "Greeting, earthlings." He waits. "That's your line," he instructs when I don't respond.

"I'm not saying that."

"Yes, you are."

"Am not."

Mandy chuckles. "You two are so cute together."

David must have stepped on her foot in warning because she squeals. I don't mind the observation. The slow smile coming to life on Joey's face says he doesn't either. His eyes are sparkling, even more so then usual. It's like they are illuminated from within, a physical sign to his strong Christian faith. "Eyes of a Believer" I once heard them described as.

"Fine," I hold up my hand in the tricky position. My *Star Trek* loving brother has long since taught me how to make the formation. "Greetings, earthlings."

"That's my girl," Joey approves, grin widening.

I blush. *Wow, I blush a lot in his presence. Thank goodness he can't see it.*

But Mandy and David can. Mandy smirks, as if to say it will only be so long before we are labelled as something deeper then friends.

In the next minutes, the couple listen, offering helpful tips as Joey coaches. David laughs the loudest when I pop the wrapped piece of gum in my mouth, perfectly in ignorant alien character when Joey fails to mention I need to unwrap the gum first.

"Then you flatten the gum over the end of your tongue and blow. Like the gum is a balloon that your breath is filling with air."

I follow Joey's last direction and blow. The first two attempts fail but you know what they say about a third time being a charm...

"I got it!" I cry out, way too happy with my triumph to care that I have splattered chewed gum sticking to my face, courtesy to a popped bubble. "My first bubble!"

Joey loosens his black tie, smirking. His black suit jack is slung around the back of his seat. "Must have had a talented teacher."

"Or maybe I'm just a natural." I tease back, loving how Joey makes me feel at ease and comfortable enough to joke. I feel like I can be myself with him. Flaws and all.

"Maybe, but I doubt it."

We gather our sub wrappings and empty cups and stand to leave. We've been here for almost two hours. An afternoon movie is on the possible next event for the group.

I look around at the group after we toss our garbage out. Joey is holding the door open for David and Mandy. The couple are holding hands. *What a wonderful surprise, multiple new friendships.* I follow David and Mandy out into the sunlight. We split into two cars, Joey riding shot gun with me. *It shouldn't surprise me. I asked for this.* I've been praying for people to help encourage healing of the scars left on my mind from my eating disorder days. And today is evidence.

That God is listening loud and clear.

***

"You and Joey are spending a lot of time together."

It's the following Thursday. I'm walking with my aunt and Jack to the grocery store for milk, so we can have cereal for breakfast.

"We get along." I don't elaborate but I know it's obvious there is something deeper going on. We've established a bit of a routine. I make the ten minute walk to work each day (occasionally borrowing Uncle Randy's old bike, making the commute four minutes), work my shift until three, walk home, change, then meet up with Joey at the church around four, where he is usually finishing up for the day himself. We spend an hour together, laughing, Joey trying to teach me piano, or playing fetch with Mac on the church front lawn. More often than not, we go out for supper together then watch a movie or take Mac for a walk. One night I joined the Waterloo's for supper. It was really nice to experience Joey interacting with his family. He's just as joyful, kind, and friendly with them as he is with his friends.

Aunt Jill casts a knowing look but doesn't comment and I'm glad. A heart to heart can be in the future. But not now with Jack tagging along.

"I like Joey," Jack declares. "He's funny."

"Do you miss your piano lessons?" I ask, grabbing Jack's hand as we cross the street. He's too old to need the guidance but we both like the familiar routine from past summers and vacations.

"Mostly the candy he gives me afterwards."

"Oh, Jack." Aunt Jill rolls her eyes.

We step inside the store. Thursday's are late night shopping night. Typically, the grocery store is crazy busy on Thursdays. Strangely, not tonight.

Aunt Jill grabs a green basket. "I just remembered a few more things I need for the BBQ tomorrow."

Jack pumps his fit, jumping into the air. "Barbeques are the bee's knees!"

I stop in my tracks and frown. "What did you just say?"

"He's been talking to his Grandpa on the phone," Aunt Jill explains, spying sesame seeded hamburger buns in the bakery section. She lifts them from the shelf and places them in her basket. "I wouldn't put it past Randy's father to pay Jack to try and get slang from back in his day back in rotation."

"Yup! Two whole dollars!" Jack chirps in. "Grandpa's awesome." He makes the cutest face ever, frowning in concentration. "He's the cats PJ's."

"I think you mean the cat's pajamas," I ruffle his wild hair. "But close enough. E for effort."

We slowly make our way down the next aisle. Jack places a package of gummy bears in the cart, chatting excitedly about soccer camp starting up soon.

Aunt Jill promptly retrieves the candy. "Think about your teeth, child. I'm the one who will have to pay for cavity damage."

So Jack's sense of humor isn't just from his father's side. Jack wrinkles his nose at his mom but doesn't argue. He's a good kid, respecting authority figures, even if his shoulders slump slightly. "Who's coming to the BBQ?" I ask, taking the basket from Aunt Jill when we step up to the deli, so she can inspect the ground beef to make homemade patties.

"Mostly families from church. " Her eyes hold a glint of mischief. "The Waterloos said they're coming."

My interest peaks. My stomach gets a fluttering feeling, deep in the pit. *Oh, dear. Is this going to be a regular occurring feeling?* But who am I kidding? I don't mind lurching, sea sick, yet wonderful feeling that appears whenever Joey comes up in the conversation.

And that is a truth no lie could ever disguise.

***

Peanut butter. The enemy.

It's Friday, the day of the backyard BBQ. Currently, it's around eleven am and I'm still at the restaurant. I'm regretting my breakfast choice. Peanut butter was one of my "bad feeling" trigger foods. I've avoided it for over a year, giving up my favorite food in order to reduce the risk of feeling regret and guilt. But today, an all-consuming guilt is my constant companion, attacking me with obsessive thoughts. I'm struggling to not head to a bathroom stall and curl up in a ball and cry out to God for mercy from my own warped thoughts.

"Hi there. Can I start you off with some drinks?" I paint on a smile, setting two menus down at my next table. I scribble the elderly couple's response down, glad for a paper to record it on. I'm way too distracted and hungry to even remember two drinks. As it is, I've messed up multiple orders.

By the time two pm rolls around, I'm stick to my stomach. Skipping lunch isn't something I've practiced in a while. Nearly eight months, I think. But today I gave into the impulse. The lie. That I would feel better, thinner, by punishing myself for a high calorie food choice.

Mentally, I've brought to mind all the fatty foods I've eaten lately, multiple times throughout the day. *Last Friday's pizza... chocolate covered almonds yesterday... full fat salad dressing... shredded cheddar cheese on my taco salad last night...*

I try to focus on my end of shift closing duties. But the empty ache in my stomach demands to be acknowledged. *How can I feel strong willed and powerful but at the same time so weak?* Regret painfully twists in my gut, working its way into an anxiety attack. My body aches and I'm tempted to go find Advil from my purse. Physical symptoms of stress, like muscle soreness, are familiar to me from the worst of my eating disorder days. A sense of failure washes over me, from what I relapsed into today.

I never wanted to go back to this place, God. You said I never had to go back! I can't drag myself to the bathroom for privacy, but I can pray right in the middle of the nosy restaurant. God can hear me from anywhere.

Words from last night's Bible reading come back to me. I was reading *The Message*, a paraphrased version of the Bible in common day speech. I can't remember the exact reference but the passage said that nothing I ever do will change God's love for me. He will never love me less or more, no matter what choices I make. His love simply remains. Joey told me the same thing a couple of days ago.

I smile a fake greeting as a group of lawyers, who visit regularly for afternoon coffee, come into the restaurant. I seat them and serve them coffee, leaving dessert menus behind. Then I start rolling silverware in napkins. *God's love remains, even in a relapse, a bad choice, Cara,* I tell myself over and over. I continue reminding myself of this truth, using Joey's advice to use God's powerful voice to override the lies.

I move on to wiping down the empty tables, refilling ketchup bottles, checking the temperature of our daily soup pots in the kitchen, sanitizing the menu stack, filling the ice machine by the pop dispenser and finally, restocking the fridge with juice and a jug of chocolate milk.

"I'm off," I announce at three, untying the ends of my short black waitress apron, my notebook and pencil still inside the front pouch.

"See you!" Aleesha, a cheerful high school student with a long swishy black pony tail and face caked full of makeup, answers. She's still sorting her receipts and figuring out her tips at the back table in the staff room. Somehow, I'd done my cash out in record time. I'm amazed all my final checks were equal.

Sliding my oversized black sunglasses on, I grab my purse and head out the front door. I avoid my uncle's office. He'll know how my day's been without me saying a word. I don't feel like talking about it, at least not to him.

The ten minute walk home takes forever today. I walk like I've aged thirty years and I feel it. I'm just so tired and angry at myself.

My phone beeps. It's a text from Joey. "Want to get slushes before the BBQ?"

"No," my answer hurts. I want to see him. Being with him is relaxing. But I don't want to see him in the setting of food, even though I will at the BBQ later today. "I'm still full from lunch." The lie is sent before I can decide against it.

"Okay," he texts back. "Another time. See you in a while."

I turn my phone to silent and slide it into the pocket of my long black cardigan. *Why did I have to eat that? I wouldn't be feeling so fat today if I'd had plain toast or just butter on it. Peanut butter might be a healthy source of fat but it's so high in calories.* I'd even had the box of Shreddies cereal out, a bowl in my hand, when Jack sleepily walked into the kitchen, rubbing his eyes. His blond hair was a mess, his Spider Man top on backwards, the tag sticking out at the front near his neck.

With eyes half closed, my little cousin had taken the peanut butter from the cupboard, twisted the green lid off, stuck his finger in, and then scooped a big helping out before sucking his fingers clean. Wordlessly, he'd headed back to his room. I'm still not certain he was fully awake. The peanut butter just smelled so good, too impossible to resist.

I sigh, frustrated with my choice. Even more frustrated that a food, a non-living object, could wreak havoc on me. All day I've bullied myself, calling myself names. It's scary how easily horrible habits can make themselves at home again.

Use rational thoughts, like your counselor taught you, I instruct myself when I'm a block from home. *You have no certainty that a different breakfast would make you feel any different today.* Another rational thought: *Peanut butter with sliced bananas on flax bread and a glass of milk was a healthy choice.*

I use my key and let myself in. I sit down at the island, head on the table. Joey was right. It's my view of myself that's the problem. Not my appearance, weight or food choices. I've had "perfect" eating days before, complete with an hour long tough workout, and still felt this insecure afterwards. Yes, the thing that needs a makeover is me. The inside me. How I define beauty and view my body. How I see the reflection in the mirror. I need to replace seeing myself as "heavier" into now being "healthier".

I head to the shower to get ready to meet Joey at the church. He's working on a special music for church and won't mind if I'm slightly late. I turn on the heat as hot as I can tolerate, despite the scorching heat outdoors. The water burns my skin, barely manageable. I like it, the steam soothes me. I imagine my regrets, sense of failure and destructive thoughts sliding from my skin, swirling down the drain. But not gone forever. At least not today.

Why do I work so hard to match culture's definition of beauty? To impress people I don't even know? I lather my hair with orange scented shampoo. Conversations with Joey have made me come to some conclusions. Primarily, that the people I love don't care what I look like. I myself don't choose my friends based on looks. The people I pick to spend my life with are based on how they make me feel, how they speak to me and treat others.

What a simpler life I would lead if I could learn to focus on being someone I enjoy being. If I could just accept my healthy body.

My mind strays to Joey, never too far of a thought away. *What if it's a universal truth? What if people's outer appearance fade with time, like Joey's lack of sight has for me?* I still notice it, but it's just something that's there, not a big deal. The guy inside, his fun personality and loving nature take over, holding my attention instead.

I finish my shower and get ready. As I pull out from the curb in my car ten minutes later, I compare my previous thoughts to a movie I watched during a birthday party sleepover. We'd watched *Win a Date with Tad Hamilton*. One of the characters had been described as "dreamy" by all of us giggling teens. The actor was portraying a movie star in the movie. I was infatuated with him. But then the character's true colors began to show. His ugly colors. Suddenly, the protagonist's best friend, scrawny, plain and quiet, had seemed far more attractive. Because of how he treated his love interest. It had nothing to do with his actual looks but he was definitely better looking to me than the other character by the end. I ponder this epiphany the rest of the way to the church, praying that one day I might be able to be free of bad days like today.

And be free to eat peanut butter.

Chapter 5

"God's love remains, no failure makes Him love you less, Cara," I remind myself, clicking the lock button on my keyless entry. I swing my lanyard, housing my keys, as I walk slowly to the church doors. The thought is true, even if my heart still feels like a failure for taking a step back today.

"Hey," I find Joey in his office, eyes closed, listening to worship music. I sit down in the chair across from him.

He swivels in his chair to mute the speakers behind his desk. "Hey, how's it going?" Now he's facing me, eyes lighting up. His dark hair looks slightly mused but completely charming. I wish he was standing, so his tall frame could make me feel safe and small, like I do on our walks.

"Alright," I say. "Are you all finished?"

"Yeah, special music has all the kinks worked out. I was just listening to new releases from some Christian artists. I'm considering bringing it to the worship team and using it for next week's worship package." He leans back in his chair and watches me.

I squirm.

He knows.

"How was your day, really?"

A pause. "Not the greatest," I finally admit. "I was struggling."

"I had a feeling." He stands, guiding himself using his desk and finds his way to the chair beside me. "I had a dream last night that I was praying for you. Then I woke up around six this morning, feeling like you really needed prayer in real life."

Six, the time I would've been eating breakfast. "Does God do that often?"

"What?" Joey asks, arm around the back of his chair, chest towards me.

"Put people on your heart to pray for, exactly when they need it?"

"Yeah, He does." Joey reaches out towards his desk. Running his hands over a stack of papers, with slight raised braille bumps, his hand finds what he's looking for. A Bible. "Sometimes I know what they need prayer for specifically. Other times, I just get this sense that they need some prayer because they are having a rough time."

I've been a Christian almost my whole life, raised in a God loving family from birth. I asked Jesus into my heart at the age of four. But I still have my doubts some days. Not about the existence of God or how the world came to be, but other things. "Do you believe there is power in prayer?"

"One hundred percent." Joey goes on to tell me of an incident where he was in university, still pursuing his engineering degree. "In the middle of a lecture, I had this overwhelming sense to drop everything and pray for one of my basketball teammates. So I grabbed my books and backpack and left mid-lecture." Joey explains he found a bench outside and prayed for a long time, specifically for safety for his teammate.

"Did you ever find out what was going on?" The story intrigues me, reminding me of the climax of a Hollywood film or suspense novel.

"Sometimes God reveals to me why prayers are needed. Other times, I just have to trust they are being heard and needed." He runs his fingers over the embossed gold letters of his navy Bible. "That night, my buddy phoned me up and asked if I'd been praying for him around two in the afternoon. I said I was and learned that he indeed had been in trouble. I'd specially been given a sense he needed prayer for safety. It was around two that he'd been driving with someone who fell asleep at the wheel. But my friend had been paying attention, not texting or watching the scenery. He'd been able to shout and wake the driver in time for him to swerve the car back into the proper lane."

My heart feels tight within my chest. "That story could've had a terrible ending."

"I know," Joey holds his Bible out. "But it didn't. The Bible says the prayer of an upright living person, a believer in Christ, are both powerful and effective. It's a power I have, as do you. I'm going to use it when I'm given a sense it's needed. I won't neglect my gift."

"Can I see that?" Joey hands me the Bible. "I think that passage is from the book of James." I flip to the right chapter and find the section he is referring to. "I definitely needed prayer then. I started to feel those prayers near the end of my shift. That's when I remembered your advice to use God's voice to override the lies and that God won't love me less for a day full of poor choices." I tell him about my day, knowing it's not a healthy thing to hide.

"Aww, Cara, I'm sorry," he pulls me into a hug. It's the first time I've been enveloped in his strong arms. They're lean but muscular, courtesy of a dedication to weight lifting. Wearily, I rest my face against his blue button down dress shirt. It feels good to not have to carry this day alone. I'm so thankful God provided me with this friendship.

From above my head, I hear him whisper. "You were right. No bad choice will make God love you any less. Absolutely nothing. He's omnificent. Today didn't surprise Him."

When Joey releases me from our hug, I straighten. "The Bible talks about one of Jesus' disciples having a thorn in his side." This is something I've struggled with for a while. "Why won't Jesus remove my thorn? Free me completely from my anxiety over my looks?"

He doesn't answer right away. The trait of the wise. "Maybe because you are more useful to Him broken."

Huh. I've never thought about that way. "Like my struggles today and my past can help others?"

"Exactly. I know my own thorns remind me of my need of Jesus. And they connect me to others, since they see I'm not some perfect pastor's kid but a human like them, who makes mistakes."

"What are some of your thorns?" Shocked at my question, I rush on. "Sorry, that was way too personal to ask."

Joey reaches for me, finding my face. Gently, he cups the side of my face. "I think we're way past becoming personal, Cara."

I close my eyes, savoring the feel of our connected skin. "You feel good."

"Not as good as you." His long fingers find my hair, tangling themselves in my messy blond curls. "My thorn appears in various forms. Depending on the season of life I'm in. Like I said before, sometimes I define my blindness as a limitation and let it distract me from living life. But lately, I'm struggling with pride. My marks are down in my seminary classes, even though I'm trying." His fingers feel wonderful, like they were created to explore my curls. "I feel like as a pastor's child, I should always have profound answers on Biblical matters."

"Joey, that's ridiculous," I murmur, learning closer, eyes closing.

"So is thinking you're not absolutely stunning, Cara."

Our lips finally touch. So softly. So slowly and delicate. One hand goes to his chest, my arm around his neck. The kiss is sweet, answering questions yet creating more.

Finally, our noses brush, our breathing synchronized. "I've been wanting to do that for a while," Joey murmurs, eyes still closed.

I pull away first then touch his cheek. "I thank God for you each night, Joey."

"So do I." His eyes are open now, full of fondness built upon honesty and trust. "You're so amazing, Cara. And you don't even know it. The way you love and laugh."

"And your faith, Joey. It's so attractive to me. The way you live your life, it's apparent how much you love God and others."

"Funny how the things we find attractive in each other aren't physical, isn't it?"

He's right. And if I were to be honest, the qualities on my list for a future husband only contain non-physical traits, such as attractively strong faith, a good listener, trustworthy, confident and funny. Someone who needs and leans on me, but also leads and challenges me.

All qualities Joey possesses.

We stay in his office a few more minutes, not saying much. Just enjoying the comfortable silence.

"We should head out. I'm assuming it's getting close to five-thirty," Joey says later. "I forgot to put my watch on this morning."

I glance down at mine. "Yeah, we could leave. Being a little early won't hurt." We say a quick hello to his dad in his office across the building. He's planning to be a bit late for the BBQ. Then we chat a few minutes with the grey haired secretary, then with the janitor sweeping the entry. Like always, Mac had accompanied Joey on the walk to work. We find him chasing his tail outside. A professionally trained adult dog but still a playful puppy at heart.

"Want to walk to my house to drop Mac off, then come back for your car?" Joey asks after calling Mac over. "Since it's so nice out?"

I check my watch. "We probably have time." I watch Joey clip Mac's leash into place and then we head towards the sidewalk. I never have to say "Watch your step" or "There's a car to your left." Whenever we walk, Mac's with us and takes care of guiding Joey safely.

"That's one thing I miss," Joey shares as we walk the fifteen minutes to his house. "My licence."

"Four years without it must seem like a lifetime." My arm is looped through his, our pace slow.

Sigh. "Yeah, but I try not to dwell on it." I'm glad there is another side to Joey, aside from his awesome funny guy routine. It's refreshing to meet a guy who will open up and be honest about his trials. To share hurts and flaws. "At least I can still get around since Kindersley is a small town. Getting Mac two years ago really gave me back some more independence."

We talk about the process of attaining a Seeing Eye dog. Joey had to take a medical examination and be involved in some intense interviews, making sure he would benefit from owning a Seeing Eye dog and that it would be safe for him to have one. I was surprised to learn Mac didn't cost him anything, just the price of food and vet bills. And apparently, only seventy- two percent of dogs, from the school Mac was trained at, make it through training to graduation. The five month training period is rather tough.

When we reach the Waterloo's house, I wait outside with Mac as Joey heads inside to change from his work clothes. I pet Mac, both of us sitting on the step. The sun feels good on my skin.

A goofy grin. I'm replaying our unexpected kiss in my mind.

When Joey opens the front door, he's holding a bouquet of roses, from the garden. "Thought we could take these to your aunt and uncle's."

"Aunt Jill will love them." I take them from him, noting his blue and white plaid long sleeve and brown shorts. His black talking watch is on his wrist now. "Ready?" He keeps the door open for Mac. The golden retriever gives us a longing look before trotting inside. Every moment apart from his best friend is hard. He's not needed tonight. I'll be Joey's guide on the way back to the church.

"Yup." We head back the way we came and I sneak a look up at him, loving both the feel of our arms looped and how small and safe he makes me feel with his height. His attractiveness hits me, like it's the first time I've seen him.

By the time we make it back to the church and get my car, we have exactly seven minutes to get to the BBQ for the official start time. When we pull up, a few other people I recognize from church are just getting out of their vehicles. A few are already parked by the curb.

Joey greets all of them by name and I smile politely. They call me by name though, having heard about Randy and Jill's niece staying with them for the summer.

Inside we find a feast spread out, buffet style on the kitchen island. Juicy wedges of watermelon, large glass bowls of creamy potato salad, colorful trays of raw vegetables with dip, a slow cooker on hot pads with Uncle Randy's special sweet and sour baked beans, various condiments, paper plates, cups, and cutlery, hamburger buns and a dish of dill pickles. A section big enough for a plate of hamburgers is the only bare surface. There's a jug of iced tea, mixed with half lemonade on the counter. It's my uncle's favourite, an Arnold Palmer, named after a professional golfer who was known for ordering the concoction at restaurants. Around here, we never drink just plain iced tea.

"Hey, you two," Aunt Jill says, stepping inside from the patio french doors. "Just in time. Burgers will be done in five minutes."

"These are from my mom's garden," Joey says, handing her the bouquet.

Aunt Jill takes a big whiff and slowly exhales. "Ah, these are gorgeous. Tell your mom thanks."

"Will do."

We head outside to the backyard and mingle with the rest of the guests. Most people don't introduce themselves to

Joey at the start of a conversation. But he must recognize their voices, from being around them at church since childhood. He introduces them to me and I try to keep all their names straight.

"Okay, folks!" Uncle Randy claps his hand, gaining the attention of the cluster of families circulated around the manicured back yard and deck. "We can eat. Jill, would you mind saying grace?"

"Sure," my aunt wraps her arm around her linebacker sized husband, closing her eyes. "Heavenly Father, we thank You for all the families that could share this meal with us. Bless our conversation and bless this food to our bodies. Amen."

The families with small children head inside to plate up first. I'm starved when it's my turn in the buffet line. I grab two paper plates from the stack. Suddenly, I feel awkward. *Am I supposed to offer to help Joey plate up?* I decide to ask, risking an offence. There are people behind us and I don't have time to debate. "Umm, do you want me to tell you the options?" I hand him a plate.

"That would be great."

Relief washing over me at choosing right, I name off each dish as we pass it. A few minutes later we find a spot together on the grass. I run inside and get us each a plastic cup of Arnold Palmer and our forgotten cutlery.

When I return, Joey has struck up a conversation with a little blond haired girl. She looks around five years old. She's wearing a pink spaghetti strap dress with a daisy on the front. An identical flower is on the side of her headband. Her hair hangs in long waves, evidence of a day spent playing outside.

"Cara, this is Sara Mae," Joey explains when he senses me sitting down next to him. "She just started taking piano lessons with me this year."

The adorable beauty holds out her hand. "Hi, Cara. You're pretty."

I take her hand, my heart melting at her manners. "Hi, Sara Mae. Thank you."

From across the lawn, I see a young woman holding a baby watching us. I smile at her, feeling certain it's Sara Mae's mother. *Likely used to her outgoing daughter needing a watchful eye.*

"Sara Mae and I are going to do special music together next week at church, isn't that right?" Joey asks the girl, making a funny face.

She giggles. "You're silly, Joey."

The child is beyond lovable. "I can't wait to hear it! What song are you going to play?" I ask.

Sara Mae does a little twirl, holding out the sides of her dress. She looks like a princess trying not to trip, descending down a staircase. "My favouritest song in the whole wide world."

"And what's that?" I dip a baby carrot into the pool of ranch on my plate.

"Jesus Loves Me," Sara Mae happily sighs. "It's just so pretty and my mommy sings it to me every night." She looks over at the young woman I spotted before. "I love her so much. I think I'll go sit by her now." The child reaches for my free hand and shakes it. "It was very nice to meet you, Joey's pretty friend."

I laugh, humored that she'd forgotten my name. "It was wonderful to meet you as well, Sara Mae. I'm looking forward to special music next week."

Skipping, Sara Mae finds her way to her mother. I watch her take a bite of a hamburger then set it down when she spots some children her age playing with bubbles. After only a few seconds of being seated, she's off running towards the fun.

"She's adorable."

"Do you want kids?"

I watch Sara Mae and the others giggling as they chase the bubbles. "Someday. I think they would be a lot of work but so rewarding."

"Me too. A house full of chaos would be great."

I pick up my hamburger and bite into it. Maybe it's because my last meal was nearly twelve hours ago but it tastes like the best burger I've ever eaten. Aunt Jill makes amazing homemade burgers. It must be one of the spices she uses. I'll have to ask her about it.

I finish my entire plate and end up going back for seconds of potato salad and watermelon. Joey requests more snap peas and cauliflower. We visit with a few other families, including a few young adults that I've met a few times before. Mandy is there with her family, David his typically quiet self at her side.

After frozen yogurt popsicles have been eaten, plates cleared and mosquito spray heavily applied to the children, Joey and I offer to take the four kids still at the party to the park across the street. Jack is one of them.

"Watch your step, there's a curb you need to go over," I tell Joey, our arms once again looped. I could get used to this. A necessity but an enjoyable one. I like being close to him. I may be supporting him but he still makes me feel secure. He's dependant on a guide at times but so very independent in many ways. I'm learning communication about potential obstacles is essential when guiding him.

"Thanks," Joey says as we step onto the grass of the school yard. The kids run ahead, excited about the playground. I stop near a bench. Usually, if it was just Jack and I, I'd be up on the play center with him, hanging from the monkey bars and swinging on the tire swing. But tonight he has playmates. And I have a bench that would make a perfect conversation spot with a certain someone.

"Let's sit," I suggest, moving us closer to the bench.

Joey follows my lead. I watch as the kids start up a game that they all know the rules for, without saying a word. My best guess is its Grounders. A game where one person has to walk around on the sand with their eyes closed. If they say "grounders" when someone else is not on the playground, that person becomes "it".

It makes me think of something. "Would it be weird if one day I wanted to experience what you do? Even for an hour?"

"To be blind?"

"Yeah, like with a blindfold."

Joey thinks about it. "If you want to. It would be quite the shock."

"I want to experience what you do on a daily basis."

He moves in closer and pretends to stretch, ending with his arm around me. A classic move. He grins, knowing I'm onto his little act. "If you want to, then sure. We just might need someone else around, for safety reasons. I bet Erica and her boyfriend would be game. Or maybe Mandy and David." I snuggle closer to him, glad he didn't think my idea was stupid. Erica had to work tonight at a sporting good's store. I'd visited it once earlier in the summer, when I was browsing the shops down Main Street. I don't recall seeing her there then.

"I want to meet Erica and Isaac soon." Her boyfriend is from India. They met at the University of Saskatchewan, where they both are majoring in biology. The Saskatoon campus is so large, I'm surprised if I see a familiar face when I walk to my next class. I might have passed them in my two years attending and just not realized it since we hadn't met.

"Yeah, she wasn't at that family dinner you joined us for."

"Nope." I watch the kids playing, wondering when I should call them in. The sunset is just showing its colors in the sky. "I wish you could see the sunset, Joey." I say without thinking. Instantly, I feel bad for bringing up something he can't ever enjoy again.

He doesn't see it that way. "Describe it to me," he says, pulling me a little closer.

I stare at the sky beyond the play center. "It has streaks of vibrant pinks at the top followed by bright oranges. There's a touch of red and I even see some purple peeking through some parts."

I lean my head on Joey's shoulder. Some may say we are acting just like the romantic comedies that Joey dislikes. But romances sometimes happen quickly. We've talked about setting boundaries. A kiss and a cuddle is as far as we will go.

"Don't feel bad for me, okay?" Joey asks of me. "I know that's what you were thinking. A lot of people tense up when they start talking about nature scenes or art work around me." His gaze is towards the sky, searching it blankly. "But I can still enjoy them through their eyes. And it's not like I've never seen a sunset in my life. I had the gift of sight for twenty years of my life. Memory is a gift from God."

His words play over in my mind as I ready for bed that night. Memories are a great thing. They help us recall past good times, allowing us to visit them on a bad day.

I turn to my side, gazing at the cherry red walls of the guestroom. But all I'm really picturing is Joey. His easy smile, the sound of his laugh and how his dark hair looks when it's windblown.

As I fall asleep that night, I know with certainty that he will be in many more good memories to come. Today may have been majority spent in anxiety but the end made up for it. My gift from God, in the form of Joey Waterloo, was the reason I felt at peace throughout the evening.

A sign that his prayers on my behalf had not fallen upon deaf ears.

***

It's not until almost two weeks later that I meet Erica. The summer is flying by and I'm desperate to cling to both the warm weather and the close living proximity I have to Joey.

I like talking to Erica, especially about our mutual love for the university campus. The U of S is breathtaking, with white cobblestone buildings and large grass areas perfect for frisbee throwing and cloud gazing. A busy but beautiful place to study, whether the trees are covered with frost or cherry blossoms.

"You and my brother make a cute couple." I'm sitting on the front step with Erica, waiting for her boyfriend, Isaac, and Joey to return with takeout. It took me only a few suppers out with Joey to realize he *really* likes Subway. Granted, there aren't many fast foods restaurants in a town of five thousand. And the part that I find hilarious? Joey doesn't even have a favourite sub. Each time we've gone, alone or with others, he tries something completely new. But the look of excitement as he stand behind the glass barrier between him and the various toppings is always the same.

Childlike excitement.

Me? I'm not so adventurous. More of a turkey and swiss on whole wheat with tomato, mayo and spinach kind of girl. Boring but the outcome is predictable: I know I'll enjoy it.

"Thanks," I say, not sure what else to say. "We've been officially dating for one week now." Joey had joined my family for a hotdog and smores supper that night. When it got late, Uncle Randy carried a sleepy Jack back into the house and Aunt Jill followed with the unused graham crackers, chocolate, marshmallows and hot dog buns. Left alone by the slowly dying fire, Joey cleared his voice, all cute and nervous and asked if I would consider being his girlfriend.

"I thought I already was," I said, inching closer to him on the wooden bench, his green army style canvas jacket draped over my bare tank top shoulders.

"Oh, just checking then, I guess." He'd looked so unlike himself, the confident man I know gone for the moment. It was a side that I found rather amusing and wouldn't mind seeing again.

"How long have you and Isaac been dating?" I ask Erica as the memory of the campfire fades.

"Since my first year of university, so about three years." Her eyes are outlined in dark liner making her chocolate eyes even more striking. She definitely has the muscular body of a heavy weight lifter. She revealed earlier it was her high school passion. She's not ultra-thin but muscular and healthy. Standing next to Joey, she's about three inches shorter than his 6'3 height. "Isaac and I are planning to go backpacking throughout Europe next summer. I'm still trying to get him to agree to find a place to bungee jump while we are travelling. Maybe at an exotic destination on the way."

I picture myself attached to a rope at the ankle, diving headfirst into a free fall over water. "I could never do that. " I shiver, just thinking about it.

"Joey and I did it a few years ago. When our family was vacationing in Fiji." She gathers her waist length dark ringlet curls into a pony tail, tying it with the elastic on her wrist. "It was his idea but I ended up loving it."

Huh. So he has a little daredevil in him. "He never mentioned that before."

Erica plucks a daisy top from the pot next to her on the step, twilling it between her fingers. "It was just before the accident. Sometimes he avoids talking about events that happened close to that basketball game. Even though I tell him it's not his fault and he accepts that fact, I can see it in his eyes sometimes. A longing to go back in time and change choices. I think it just hurts to remember those painful years of relearning everything." She tosses the flower aside. "It helps when I mention that maybe God intended him to become blind, that he could be used more powerfully in the lives of others that way."

It sounds like something Joey would say to me. Actually, it sounds a lot like one of our conversations about thorns, why I still struggle with body image. "He's pretty positive and insanely independent."

"Obviously he can't choose some career paths, like a pilot. But he can certainly do most of what anyone else can, just differently." The boys are pulling up into the driveway. Isaac's driving Erica's silver Honda. "He's a trooper and it shows. His faith got him through those tough years. It's stronger now than ever, an inspiration to me." We both stand and greet the boys.

I like Erica. She's deep like Joey. Maybe not as goofy, but her love for her brother and others is crystal clear. I took an assertiveness class in high school and the teacher told us to ask ourselves to picture an assertive, strong and confident person we knew. Then we were instructed to visualise what that person would do in the tricky situation we were in. I hadn't known Erica then, but now if I'm struggling between being passive and afraid of hurting feelings, I will picture her and try to replicate what she would say if she were in my situation.

"Grub's here!" Joey says, slamming the car door then holding up three long plastic individual bags of subs. Erica's chicken vegetable chopped salad is in Isaac's hand, as are our drinks. Next to Isaac, Joey 6'3 looks almost small. Even from a distance, Isaacs near seven feet height seems to loom. I don't even have to ask if he plays for the U of S Huskies basketball team. The coaches would probably *pay* him to play!

Since it's nice out, we decide to take our food to the backyard. The Waterloo's have a gazebo, with green spidery vines intertwined between the white lattice. The entire backyard could be a florist shop. It's no wonder Aunt Jill and Joey's mom are so talkative after church services. Their mutual green thumbs are obvious. Though my aunt is more into vegetable gardening then flowers.

"Subway. Like modern day manna," Joey murmurs, inhaling the scent of his subs as he unwraps it.

I roll my eyes but love the creative comparison. Only Joey would think to compare his favourite food to the food God provided for the Israelites in Biblical days, the bread raining daily from the sky.

The conversation is lively, as most are when Joey is with friends. Our one on one conversations tend to be deeper but I know Joey has them with others, too. It's common for an unexpectant hurting stranger to stop by the church during the week and end up pouring their struggles out to one of the pastors. Joey's office is closest to the front door and gets the majority of it. Sometimes, he calls his dad to come join in the conversation but sometimes he just does it on its own. And Joey loves it. Listening to people's hurt and relying on God to give him words of wisdom.

"Were you born here, Isaac?" I ask Erica's boyfriend. He doesn't have an accent, his English perfect.

Isaac finishes chewing a bite of sub then shakes his head. "I was born in New Delhi, India's capital. We moved here when I was seven."

"Do you miss it?"

"I've been back to visit family a few times. They're what I miss most."

You learn a lot from a couple by watching how they interact. I watch as Erica's smile lights up around Isaac and how he keeps looking down at her, adoration in his eyes.

"An engagement in the making," Joey told me last night over bowls of popcorn at the theater. "Mark my words."

Just looking at them, I don't doubt it. But they never make me feel uncomfortable. No awkward kissing, not even holding hands. Just the look in their eyes is the evidence that they're in love.

After supper is done, we break out a board game of Apples to Apples. I've always loved how board games act as a get to know you tool. They allow for people to talk and open up, but with a focal point of a game. Interactions aren't intimidating then, like when the focus is solely on each other.

Isaac's good for Erica. He brings out the light hearted side of her. He teases her about her slow decision making on picking the best noun card in her hand, to describe the adjective card in play. "Stop rushing me!" she laughs, finally choosing and laying a red card next to the ones Joey and I have already selected. "You're stressing me out, Isaac."

"Get used to it, babe," he says, gathering the three cards to choose his favourite. He's the judge this round. "Board games are in our future and you need to learn to make fast choices. You'd make molasses cringe if it was playing with us."

Laughs all around, even more so when Erica licks her finger and puts it in Isaac's ear, twisting her finger.

"Ahhh!" Isaac squishes his ear down onto his shoulder. "I thought we agreed no more wet willies, Erica!"

"I made an executive decision and decided to scratch that settlement."

Joey and I both light up with laughter when Isaac wraps his tanned arms around Erica, ruffling up her hair, pinning her in a headlock. "You were saying?"

"Okay, okay!" Erica's laughter matches ours. "No more wet willies, I promise! Just stop messing up my hair!"

Isaac lets go and Joey gives him a look, one eyebrow raised. "Two words for next time she gets annoying: Ticklish feet."

Erica sticks her tongue out at him.

"She just stuck out her tongue at me, didn't she?" Joey doesn't wait for an answer. He sticks his tongue out at his sister.

"How old are you two?" I ask, smiling at the siblings. Isaac brings out the "Joey" in Erica.

"Twenty three," Erica admits, with a sheepish smile.

"Four, plus twenty," Joey answers, still looking at his sister. Now he's got his pinkies hooked on each side of his mouth, his tongue wiggling back and forth.

"The Waterloos are an acquired taste," Isaac says, grinning at me. "But you get used to them." His dark eyes are alive with laughter.

"Yeah, we're kind of like avocados in that way," Joey says, finally looking away from his sister, hands folded tamely on the gazebo stone table.

The topics for the rest of the night are fascinating. I learn that Erica and Isaac ran a marathon with Joey two years ago. Joey had run one before the accident but this time Isaac and Erica trained with him, guiding him through the race with their words, sometimes running backwards as they guided him from in front.

Erica and Isaac share the funny story of how they met. Isaac had just spilled Pepsi on a seat in an intro Biology class and left to get paper towel from the men's bathroom. He return to find Erica seconds from choosing that very seat.

"I was too late though, even though I started to run," Isaac says. "I was waving my arms like a mad man, and people were staring wide eyed."

"You certainty made a memorable impression that first day of university," Erica smirks. "But I forgave you. Sticky pants is a small price to pay for falling in love."

Joey gags and stands. "And that is our cue to leave, Cara."

Isaac and Erica don't even notice us leave. I'm not offended at all. I've loved spending the Friday evening with them. But every couple needs some alone time.

Speaking of which…

Joey holds out his hand and I take it, letting him lead me to the house. He knows the way, the number of round raised steps nestled into the grass, leading to the house, long since memorized.

In the kitchen, Joey leans against the counter, a playful look in his blue eyes. "What do you want to do now?"

"That depends." I lean my back against the counter next to him. "We could watch TV or go buy Mac a new toy." Joey starts tracing the lines in the back of my hand with his long fingers. It's making it rather difficult to concentrate and continue my coy routine. "Or maybe we should call it a night, I'm feeling tuckered out."

Joey comes closer the same time I do. Our faces are inches apart now. "Nah, I have a better idea," he says and then his smiling lips press down onto my own.

His hands travel to my waist and I wrap my arms around his neck. I love this boy, I really do. I haven't said it yet but I certainly feel it. There's nothing like being held in his strong arms, having him tenderly kiss away stresses of the day. The kiss deepens and feelings I've never felt before surge through my entire body. It's pure pleasure but I know it has to stop. I firmly push away, a hand to Joey's chest. "We need to take a breather."

His breath is heavy and his eyes hold a longing for more. But he nods. He understands. We've talked about this before. When one of us says it's time for a break, the other one has to take the way out of temptation the first time it's offered. "Yeah, let's go outside."

We get comfy on the front step, a now very familiar place for me at the Waterloo's residence. I've shared countless evening chats with Joey about dreams, fears and passions here.

Our fingers quickly find each other again.

"You know what another advantage of being blind is?" Joey asks, breaking into my happy thoughts of how tonight is going.

"What?"

He squeezes my hand, sending the butterflies in my stomach soaring. "I have an excuse to hold your hand more often, since I need it for guidance."

I swat him playing. "You and I both know that's not true. You don't need a guide like I don't need a curling iron."

An arm slings around me. I love the feeling. "I know but it never hurts to hold your hand extra."

"No argument there."

Dusk has arrived and twinkling white faraway stars shine overhead. "Want me to describe the stars to you?"

"Please."

I lean my head on his shoulder and gaze up at the stars. "They look like thousands of tiny white lights peaking trough a black carpet. Aunt Jill says stars are glimpses of heaven shining through."

"I like that description." I close my eyes when Joey kisses me softly on the check. "Seeing scenery through your eyes is the best. Another gift from above."

Just like you. We spend the rest of our evening silently staring into the night, holding each other and holding onto the remainder of our summer together.

***

The next day, I find myself sandwiched between Joey and Jack on a piano bench. Joey joined my family for a brunch of waffles, scrambled eggs, orange juice and fruit salad. Now he's helping Jack fine tune a number he's playing at a wedding later in the summer. Somehow, me watching from the couch turned into me being lured into a lesson.

"This is middle C," Jack says, jabbing a stubby finger at the center white key. "That's your go-to key, don't forget it."

I'm certain he's reciting words he's heard Joey say during one of his earlier lessons. I look over Jack's head of wild curls and see Joey holding back laughter. My guess is correct.

Joey's taught me a few things about piano this summer but I usually just end up getting him to play me something. There's nothing more relaxing then listening to that boy play. Whether it's a worship song or not, I can literally feel God's presence surround me as I listen to the melodies Joey creates through his fingertips. Even without a description of the story behind the song, I find myself easily transported to scenes of majestic rainforests, nighttime bandit races alongside trains or Arabian nights spent in a wide open desert.

"So this is C?" I ask, pointing to a note I know is A.

"No!" Jack giggles, reaching over me and pointing to the correct key. "This is C."

"Are you sure?" I point to B. "Maybe this is it."

Joey presses down on the B note closest to him. He leans his ear in close, concentrating. "Sounds like a C to me, Jack. She might be right."

Jack's jaw drops. "But that's a B. I know it is, deep down in my heart."

Joey ruffles his hair. Curls are hard to resist. He does the same to mine occasionally. "I know. I was just kidding."

"So it's a C?" Worry lines Jack's innocent face.

"Yes."

Jack's shoulders slouch, losing their tension. "Whew! I was questioning my memory there for a second."

The two of them teach me "Mary Had a Little Lamb" on the piano. I get pretty good and can play it by memory after a while. Then Joey gets Jack to get out his sheet music for "Here Comes the Bride". I move to the couch and watch Joey in his element, teaching his passion of piano. He listens closely as Jack plays the popular wedding song. Once Jack's hands return to his lap, Joey offers a few suggestions about playing some parts louder and some parts softer, for dramatic effect. He reminds

Jack about a sharp that comes into effect in one part of the song and corrects a note that Jack played wrong.

"And make sure you're reading the notes, not playing by memory."

"Mom keeps telling me that," Jack says looking ashamed. "I keep forgetting."

"No big deal, buddy. It just gives less power to your nerves if you don't memorize it. They might make you forget but if you can read the music, you'll be fine, even if you're nervous."

"Okay."

After Joey tells Jack to keep practicing and that it sounds really good, they call me back over to the piano. This time, the goal is to teach me "Ode to Joy". Again, I catch on pretty quickly. Eventually Jack loses interest and heads downstairs to, "Spend some quality time with the X-Box. I feel like I'm neglecting him lately."

"It feels so weird to tell my students not to play by memory," Joey confesses once it's just us on the piano bench. It's a place I've spent many hours this summer with him. Usually, at the church's grand piano but any piano feels familiar. "Since it's what I do now."

I smooth out the wrinkles of "Here Comes the Bride" sheet music. It looks like Jack crumbled it into a ball. I wouldn't be surprised if he couldn't find his baseball and pulled the music out to use for playing catch with his friends. "Do you like piano any less now that you have to play by ear?"

"No, piano will always be something I enjoy. I just have to learn songs and play slightly differently now." He tells me about how his first year of university, living away from home, he purchased a cheap keyboard because he missed playing so much. "After playing since I was five on an upright piano, it definitely sounded different. But it still allowed me to play." His face takes on a fond look of someone reminiscing a beloved time gone by. "That keyboard provided me with many hours of enjoyment."

"And hours of studying and essay writing procrastination?"

A slow smile. "However did you guess?"

I laugh. I do that more with Joey then anyone.

We talk about how piano is one of the easiest musical instruments for the blind to learn. Joey's been teaching a seven year old boy, blind from birth, to play piano.

"It's a challenge at times but it's worth it."

"How do you teach someone to play that's blind?" I really have no idea. With Joey it makes sense. The sound of the keys and position of them were engraved in his head, thanks to completing all levels of Royal Conservatory Piano way before the accident.

"We just took it slow. First, I got him to recognize middle C. Then the keys that have two or three black keys on them. Then I got him to listen to how the pitch of the notes gets either higher or lower, depending on which way you move on the piano." Joey shuts the old brown piano, covering the keys. "Once Timothy was advanced enough to benefit from it, I put raised bumps on all the C's on the piano, to orient himself whenever he lost his place."

Anyone who has ever played an instrument awes me. But someone who is blind even more so. "You must have a lot of music memorized."

"Yeah." Joey drums his fingers on the closed piano covering. "I had to memorize some of my favourites after I lost my vision. Most of them were famous pieces so I could easily find recordings of them online. Then I just listened to them over and over, picking out each note by the sound. I would stop and start the recording, play a little, memorize it, then keep repeating until I knew the song by heart."

"That's amazing."

"Not really, it's just what measure you take when you love something. You don't let it go." He reaches for my hand. I know he's referring to me but I know he gave up on piano for an entire year. When he was struggling with depression. Those first few years post-accident, he let himself believe his piano playing days were lost alongside his vision. Depression dims passions and interests, which was probably part of it too.

"Who's your favourite pianist?"

He doesn't hesitate. "A Japanese guy, Nobuyuki Tsuji. Just thinking about him inspires me." Blue eyes light up and I sense a monologue on the horizon. "The piano is like an extension of his hand. When he plays, it's truly divine, unquestionably a gift from God. He creates sounds I'm sure we'll experience in heaven."

Joey is so excited about the topic he forgets to insert periods and pauses, rushing through the explanation of his beloved piano inspiration. "I had the privilege of going to one of his concerts. It was phenomenal, like listening to an angel. He even played one of Beethoven's trickiest compositions, Sonata Number Twenty-Nine. For someone with sight to learn that piece, it's beyond impressive but for a blind person? Who learns by ear? It's just incredible." Joey's eyes take on a faraway look, as if remembering the sound. "It's an *hour* straight of insanely difficult chord combinations and notes." A head shake, and awe

100

colors his face. "But Nobuyuki played it flawlessly and in this utterly natural way. All by *memory.*"

"Wow."

"I'll say."

I listen more as Joey talks about the concert. I love the passion I hear in his voice, the way his eyes come alive and how he is with kids, sharing his joy of piano with them.

Love. We haven't said those three small words yet. But it's coming. I know it is.

"Hey, how are you?" Joey asks me later that afternoon. We are seated on top of a picnic table overlooking the water, feet on the bench. Trees provide shade from the heat of the midafternoon sun. The walking trail is busy with walkers, mothers with strollers, kids on bikes and runners. We don't even ask if we want to spend our entire days off together. It's just a given. Though it's common for us to hang out with Erica or Isaac, one of our families or go bowling with the young adults.

It's a small town, just under five thousand. Bowling is one of the few things to do for entertainment. Or a movie at the small theater, which features a single new film every two weeks. Small towns, gotta appreciate their charm!

I know what he's referring to. "I'm doing good. I still have some anxiety and negative thoughts about my body, usually in the morning, but it's alright."

"I've been praying for you, every night when I talk to God about the day."

"I know." It's just what he does. "I feel those prayers."

I'm telling the truth. Though I've avoided peanut butter and desserts lately, I haven't skipped any meals. Erica was helping me pick out runners one day at her store and we had a very helpful conversation. We'd been discussing how university session would be starting up in a month and our summer jobs would soon feel like a lifetime away. I brought up the subject of being glad swimsuit seasons would be over.

She frowned at me. "Do you struggle with that?"

I'd nodded. "Don't most girls?"

She sat down next to me on the bench, tissue paper filled open boxes spewed on the floor before us. "I used to but then I learned something. It's helped me not worry about it so much."

I started tying the laces on a navy and metallic purple shoe. "What?"

"That I would never be happy with myself, at any size, if I didn't start seeing myself differently."

The laces fell limp in my hand. "Joey told me something similar. That as humans, we always will crave acceptance. What *can* change is how we view ourselves."

"Exactly." Thinking of a beauty like Erica, a confident, independent, educated, and athletic woman, having insecurities is baffling. I guess no one's in that boat alone. Even if we pretend otherwise, we all feel it. We all compare ourselves and feel like we don't measure up. "Now I make it a conscious effort to say something nice to myself each time I look into the mirror in the morning."

I tell Joey about our conversation.

"Have you given it a shot?"

"Mmm hmm. Yesterday was, 'I like the color of your eyes'. And today's compliment was, 'Your nose is a cool shape."

The last one earns me a grin. He tweaks me on the end of my nose with his finger. "I agree. It's adorable."

Our smiling lips meet. Short but sweet.

We pull apart, both still grinning.

"I don't think I'll ever get tired of you," Joey says, finding a small pebble beside him and tossing it into the water. It splashes a moment later.

"I beg to differ," I say, savoring the feel of a weekend afternoon that seems to stretch out endless before us.

"Impossible." Joey moves to the bench, leaving me sitting solo on top. "So I asked Erica something the other day about you."

The way he says it, he sounds guilty. I slide down onto the spot next to him. "What?"

"I asked what you look like."

My stomach lurches. And not in the good way. Betrayal. Fear over what was said. Had Joey's image of me in his mind changed? For the worse?

"Relax," Joey reaches for my hand, his aviator sunglasses in place. I wish they were gone so I could see his eyes. "I only asked to illustrate something. To compare."

"I don't understand."

"I asked for your benefit, not mine. I honestly don't care what you look like. I love the girl I see inside. She's beautiful.

But I thought it might help you to hear a description. To see how others see you, without the jaded vision your have yourself." A quick squeeze of my hand. "Can you describe yourself to me, what you see in the mirror?"

Well, that would be easy. Just today, despite my self-given nose compliment, I had cringed when I caught an unflattering angle of my reflection in a car window. "Honestly? Sometimes I see a fat face, big arms and a bulging stomach. It makes me feel weak for allowing my body to gain weight, even if I know deep down it's a healthy weight."

"Cara, you run and do yoga, don't you?" He knows I do and doesn't need me to answer. I've come to meet up with him straight after a 5km run or still carrying my yoga mat after joining my aunt for her power yoga classes every Wednesday night. "And we've been going for lots of walks this summer. Even without seeing you, I'm certain you're not the overweight person you see yourself as."

"I know I'm not. It's just sometimes I feel like I'm eating so much and not exercising enough. Like I'm weak for having less strict will power, in comparison to my past. But then I try to tell myself that the old me is not a healthy role model to compare myself to. She may have weighed less but she was carrying a lot of weight of misery and pain on her shoulders. She was sick. I don't want to be her anymore."

Arm around me, a kiss on the top of my head. "That way of thinking shows your healing's still going strong."

"Besides the peanut butter incident, I haven't skipped any meals. And I don't turn to over exercising any more to feel better. I've been trying to pray through the painful days."

"That's awesome to hear. God is so good, lending us His strength to walk away from poor choices but loving us even when we don't." Joey's arms wrap tighter around me and I lean into the embrace. Could a more perfect summer moment be found? The sun has moved and now it's warming my bare skin. I'm wearing a deep blue sleeveless summer dress, white flip flops, and my air dried wild curls are spilling out of a short pony tail.

"Erica described you as pretty. She said you reminded her of Reese Weatherspoon, especially her character in *Sweet Home Alabama*, when her hair was the same length as yours."

It's not the first time I've been compared to the petite blond actress. "Reese is beautiful." I can vaguely see the resemblance, but clearly I'm not in the same category as the gorgeous starlet.

"And so are you," Joey insists. "Do you see how different your own view of yourself and Erica's are? Both descriptions create totally different images of a woman in my mind."

I gulp. Which one was true? Which one did Joey picture me as?

Joey ends the hug, turning me towards him and reaches for my face. Slowly, his hands travel across my face, first framing my face with his hands. They trace the curve of my jawline, the spot under my lips and end at my temples, making small circles on my skin. "I feel with my hands a petite face, Cara. And a face frowning because it doesn't accept itself for what it is."

I reach out and remove his sunglasses. His hands are still on my face, now cupping my cheeks. His eyes are concentrating on a spot just over my shoulder. "I'm learning that emotions, mirrors and pictures lie. Stress or a bad angle can completely change how things look. They don't always tell the truth."

"Very wise. Did your counsellor teach you that?"

"Yes, but it's only starting to sink in."

"Can I share something with you?" His hands leave my face. My skin chills without his touch. "You terrify me, Cara."

"Me? Why would I scare you?"

"Because you love me."

We said those pivotal words a week ago to each other, in his backyard. We'd been laying on our backs, after I described some of the cloud pictures I could make out in the sky to him. "Why would that terrify you?"

"Because you accept me, blindness and all. And I worry that if what we have ends, I won't find another you."

My heart melts as I watch him hang his head. Joey hates to be weak and unconfident. Advice to other's personal problems is a strength, but bringing his own insecurities to light is hard for him. I lean my head on the familiar curve of his shoulder, gazing out at the water. There's a few kayakers in the water. "I can't promise that we'll end up getting married, Joey, that we'll be a forever thing." I feel his body tense. "But what I can promise is that after spending time with you, people, no pun intended, turn a blind eye to your lack of sight. We just don't see it anymore. Or if we do, we don't care."

Joey is quiet, letting my words sink in. It's interesting how we both struggle with our outer features. Yet to one another, we see the truth. We see the trivial of appearances. We see the beauty beyond, the kind that doesn't fade with time.

Our conversation lulls. I think we both need time to process what we both said to each other. We decide to spend the evening with our separate families, feeling like we've been neglecting quality time with them. Neither of us wants to be the kind of couple who only has time for each other. Jack's been asking me to go rollerblading with him for a while. I think I'll surprise him by asking *him* tonight.

I help my aunt make supper that night. We're having omelets in a bag and fresh fruit.

I open the bag of green grapes and start to pick them from the vine to wash them. "Where's Uncle Randy?"

"At the restaurant." I'm not sure I could be a restaurant owner. "When everyone else is playing, he is working." Weekends, evenings and lunch hours are the times that Uncle Randy is needed the most. To fill in for employee shortage or to put out fires between the cooks and customers.

"He's been home quite a few suppers this summer," I note, moving to the sink with a strainer. I run water over the grapes.

Aunt Jill waits her turn to fill a big stainless steel pot with water. Zip lock bags are beside me, ready to be filled with scrambled egg mixture and the chopped vegetables, ham and shredded cheddar sitting on the counter. Eight minutes in the boiling water and the omelets will be ready to eat. "Yes, we decided it was necessary for our family. Even if it meant hiring another part time manager. Now he has Sunday's off as well and every other Friday."

"Jack needs that."

"So do I." A few short brown curls have fallen from my aunt's short pony tail. She looks tired. Jack will do that to a person, with his endless energy and enthusiasm. But she looks happy. I'm not sure how Aunt Jill does it. Raising Jack, volunteering at the church, being on the parent's board for Jack's elementary school and running a home accounting business, including managing the books for the East Side Café. A busy woman but still balanced, with conscious family time, power yoga classes and her faith to keep her sane.

Uncle Randy surprises us by making it home at six pm just as we start to fill our zip lock bags with our toppings.

"Dad!" Jack flings himself at Uncle Randy after the front door opens.

Laughing, Uncle Randy pats his son's back. "I seem to have grown an extra leg."

"You're home early," Aunt Jill hands him a bag. "It's omelet night. You're just in time."

He sets down a stack of menus. I recognize it as the new one that will start next week. He loosens his tie and then leans in to kiss my aunt's cheek. "Perfect." Aunt Jill looks instantly younger, her face lit as if a school girl in the arms of a quarterback. Fitting, since Uncle Randy could easily be mistaken for a massive linebacker. The difference in height between them is both comical and cute.

"Yuck!" Jack's hand hovers over the bowl of grated cheddar cheese. "You're not allowed to do that when I eat. I might throw up."

"One day you'll want to kiss a girl, maybe even when making omelets." Uncle Randy laughs, plucking a blueberry from the big glass bowl of fruit salad and popping it in his mouth.

"Never. Girls are gross." Realizing there are two girls near, he paints an apologetic look on his adorable, tanned, and freckled splattered face. "Except you two. You are tolerable."

I add red peppers and sliced mushrooms to my bag. Then half a handful of sliced ham. "I thought you had a girlfriend, Jack."

This gets his dad's interest. "Well, well, well. My boy, a ladies man at nine."

Jack shoots me a scowl. "That was supposed to be our secret, Cara.

I squeeze out the air from my bag and zeal it, turning to put in the pot of boiling water on the stove. "Sorry, I guess I have a big mouth. I'm a terrible cousin, maybe I should be fired." Suddenly, I feel arms wrap around my leg. I look down. Jack's face is pressed into the side of my flowered green and black shorts. "What are you doing, Jack?"

He buries his face deeper, wrapping his arms around me. "You're not a terrible cousin. You're the best. You play with me and I love you."

"Aww, Jack," Gently, I pry him off myself and kneel down next to him. His parents are quiet, watching the exchange. "I was just being sarcastic. Do you know what that is?"

"Yeah, being funny in a mean way." His lower lip is quivering and I feel like the biggest jerk in the world. I pull him into a hug. His tears come quick, spilling onto the front of my white tank top. "But I didn't think it was funny."

I hug him harder. The tiles are killing my knees but it's a small price to pay for comforting Jack. "I know, I don't anymore either."

After untangling himself from me, Jack wipes his eyes. "Promise you won't ever stop being my cousin?"

"Promise."

Relief fills his shiny eyes. "Good. You're the best that money can buy."

"Technically, I'm free but I know what you mean."

"Okay, you two, that's enough mush. There's a hungry man in this kitchen!" Uncle Randy's eyes are twinkling and he winks at me, mouthing, "Thank you." He and Aunt Jill have mentioned how they appreciate the time I spend with Jack and the interest I take in him.

Jack is about to toss his bag into the boiling water but Aunt Jill stops him. "Hold it, mister. Where are your vegetables? I see only egg, cheese and ham."

"Aww, Mom. Vegetables are nasty."

"Look at Cara's colorful omelet bag," Aunt Jill says, playing the "older cousin role model card." "Her bag is filled with vegetables. I even saw her add a second handful of peppers."

It's true. I love red peppers. "Vegetable are good for you," I tell Jack truthfully. "They help your body do cool things. Carrots help with eyesight and other vegetables can help lower your chances of getting sick, like cancer." My counsellor loaned me a book on nutrition and it helped me learn to see food as not something to be feared but as a source of useful fuel.

Jack still doesn't look convinced but reaches for the red peppers. "Okay, if you say so." He makes a dramatic show of opening his bag and placing exactly three cubes of peppers inside. "I'll eat these but mark my words, I'm not happy about it."

We all laugh and the fun evening continues past super at the oak round table, dishes and a game of Jenga. Around nine-thirty, the wind suddenly picks up. Thunder bangs through the night air, followed by a streak of lighting in the sky. Rain pours hard for an hour.

Aunt Jill hurries to finish making her chocolate chip cookies she started after Jenga, in case the power gives out. She needs them for Jack's soccer camp wind up party tomorrow.

I join Jack and Uncle Randy on the deck outside. It's chilly out and though it's thin, I'm glad for my red North Face rain jacket. "Wow, it sure got stormy fast."

Jack's eyes are wide and he stands close to Uncle Randy, one arm around his leg. "There's a tornado watch for the area," Uncle Randy looks down at Jack. "Want to go back inside with Mom, buddy?"

We've been out here awhile, watching the strong winds blow around the trees like rag dolls. The sky is an angry grey with swirls of dark storm clouds. I can hear the neighbour's wind chimes.

"I want to stay with you," Jack looks up at his dad, a Goliath sized giant in comparison to his own height. "I'm safe with you."

"That you are, buddy."

I smile at the picture they make, suddenly missing my own father. I haven't seen my parent's all summer, despite having talked to them on the phone. Both my parents were thrilled with the news about Joey and I dating. I haven't been mentally well enough for a relationship in a while, my last boyfriend being a short two month stint in grade nine. *I'll have to give them a call tomorrow after work, to catch up and say "I love you."*

My mom ends up phoning me on Wednesday around ten am. I never got around to making the call on the weekend. Today I'm working the closing late shift, so I have time to chat. We chat about Joey, my siblings, the storm and the rest of the summer. I tell her I'm looking forward to student life again but will miss this summer once it ends. She tells me about a trip to Las Vegas she and Dad are planning for fall. I listen closely, enjoying the sound of her familiar voice. The call finishes up an hour later and I tell her I love her.

"I love you too, Cara. Try to savour the rest of summer while it lasts."

"I'll try."

I'm lost in thought as I walk to work. *While it lasts.* It hits me, like a cold awakening from water, that life doesn't last forever. Bodies fade and life ends. *I need to be spending my remaining hours on important things. Like spending time with loved ones, loving God, and loving myself.*

My thoughts remain on the theme of life lasting only so long my entire shift. By the time eleven pm rolls around, I feel a sense of sadness. I perform my closing waitressing duties on autopilot. I clear and sanitize the last table of lingering guests, do my cash out, turn off the classical music station on the radio, refill the coffee beans so it's full for rush hour breakfast and turn off the restaurant dining room lights.

When I finish up, I head to Uncle Randy's office. He's working on his laptop at his desk. "All done," I say, leaning against the door frame.

"Just give me a second." He finishes saving his Microsoft Word document and then shuts down his computer. He always walks me home when I work the late shift. The route I walk is located next to a busy service road. Lots of semi drivers pull over at night and sleep on the side of the road. A few street lamps line the sidewalk, but it's still an eerie place to walk at night. Someone could easily snatch a person up and no one would even notice the kidnapping. At least that was my thought the entire time I walked home by myself one night. *Speed* walked is more like it. I would've been sprinting had it not been for the high heels.

"What's going to happen with you and Joey once summer's over?" Uncle Randy asks me as we start the walk home. It's chilly out and I hug myself.

"Long distance, I guess." Saskatoon isn't that far by car. Two hours if traffic's slow.

"Those are hard. Your aunt and I did that in our early years."

"Any advice?'

"Don't do it."

"Helpful."

A grin. "I thought so." He shoves his big hands into his grey dress pants. "The solution that finally worked for me was proposing."

"Seriously?"

"Yup. Lucky for us, the right time for that was only after a year of long distance."

Thoughts of long distance and life's shortness keep me up that night. Even a text from Joey doesn't cheer me up.

"Hope your day was great!" it says, followed by a smiley face emoticon. His classes are getting busy, lots of essays requiring hours of research piling up. With me working a lot of night shifts this week, it makes for not a lot of time to spent together. But that's okay. We'll survive. We are planning to join Erica and Isaac at the travelling amusement park Sunday night. It's something to look forward to.

"Right back at you!" I type back, knowing the sound of the text arriving won't wake him. That boy could sleep through any alarm or natural disaster. Hurricane, tsunami, earthquake, you name it.

As I lay awake, staring at the ceiling, I think about life. How I'm spending mine.

Just yesterday we had a new waitress start. She's pretty but clearly struggling. I wish I wasn't assigned to train her. I heard the tiny blond throwing up in the bathroom yesterday and again today. Both times I had seen her eating beforehand.

I know it's wrong what she's doing, harming her body like that. I know I'm in healthier place and happier but it's still hard. I'm envious of her emancipated body. A part of me still sees that as beautiful, something to be jealous of.

She's a nice girl, freshly graduated from high school this year, but I don't like to be around her. It makes me feel bad about myself. Correction, I *let* it make me feel bad. I'm the one doing the comparisons. "There is no win in comparison, nothing beneficial gained from it," I whisper to the dark room. I really don't want to find myself on my death bed, regretting all the times I wasted comparing my body to younger versions of me and other's bodies. I want to lay there remembering the joy I felt in life and the joy I brought to others.

God, I pray as sleep quietly creeps in. *Help me to achieve that joy goal. Help me to stop comparing but to see myself as good enough, as I am today. Help me to spend my remaining hours of life living the abundantly full and free life you designed for humans. Help me to redefine my definition of beautiful and to focus more on working on the inside appearance, as oppose to the outside one. Like the Bible says, beauty fades but a person's soul is what will be remembered forever. It's what's worth striving to maintain, not a body that will soon die and be easily forgotten. Help me to care more about the description on my tombstone then the size of my thighs or the number on the scale. Help me to care more about the legacy I will leave behind of how I lived life and loved others. Help me, God, help me.* Words run out and I pray myself to sleep, like I have countless times this summer.

In the morning, I wake to a robin chirping outside my window and sunlight streaming in through the slits of the white blinds. I sit up, wiping the sleep from my eyes. Today I'm working the early shift. I cast a quick glance at my alarm clock and then throw the covers off.

It's seven-thirty.

My shift began at seven. Usually, I'm up at six on opening days.

A quick call to the restaurant eases my frantic stress, slightly. There was another server, Mike, scheduled to open with me. "Take your time but hurry," he says. "It's not busy yet but will likely pick up soon."

I slip on a black flowy dress, throw on a teal dangly neckless, run my finger through my wild curls, rush through my make-up routine, grab a granola bar and apple to eat on the way, and rush out the door.

I arrive at the restaurant at exactly eight am. There are three tables occupied, two people at each.

"I'm so sorry!" I tell Mike, tossing my apple core into the garbage in the kitchen.

He looks up from pouring a cup of coffee. "Hey, it happens. We've all slept in before. My first week, I didn't show up until two one day."

I smile. "That day must have flown by since closing is at three for early shift."

"I stayed late that day." He finishes pouring a second cup of coffee and sets it next to the first on the black circular tray. "If you want to take table seven off my hands, that would be great. Seat one ordered the Grand Slam Breakfast and seat two wants French toast, no whip cream, extra blueberries."

"Sure thing." And just like that my whirlwind of a day begins. When Joey, Mandy, and David waltz in around one-thirty, I'm exhausted. Seeing them reenergizes me.

"I've got table three," I tell Mike, grabbing a few menus. "It's my boyfriend."

Mike looks up from polishing silverware. He squints. "Is that Joey Waterloo?"

"Yup."

"Good guy. I went to high school with him. We played basketball together in university too. "I don't ask but he nods, sensing the unspoken question. "I was there that day. I was the one who passed him the breakaway ball that changed things."

I put a hand to his shoulder. "Not your fault. A pass to a teammate was all it was, Mike."

"Yeah. Some days I tell myself otherwise though."

"Don't. It's not helping anyone thinking that way."

He smiles sadly and then continues polishing.

I walk up to the table of my friends. *Why is it so easy to see the flawed and warped way of other's thinking, yet not be able to get past my own thinking some days? About the shape of my body?* It's like I'm blinded by my own perception of myself, my own unhealthy standards.

I push the thought aside. "Hey guys! What can I get you to drink?" I forgot they were coming in. Joey mentioned that he would be stopping by on lunch with Mandy and David this week. They are both volunteering with kid's ministry this year. Today they are going over some music for the summer Bible camp starting in August at the church. Despite his quiet nature, David is actually an outgoing guy with high school students and a great singer. Mandy plays acoustic guitar and sings as well. Her voice is deep and country like, similar to the lead singer of the country group Lady Antebellum. I've heard them play a special music at church this summer and it was stunning. Their voices complement each other beautifully, like they were created to be intertwined.

"Coke for me!" Mandy says, taking the top menu from the stack.

"Root Beer," David requests and Joey orders an Arnold Palmer. He's in love with the drink ever since he tried the iced tea and lemonade concoction at the BBQ. I'm surprised Uncle Randy doesn't have it listed on the menu as an option. Most waitresses would have given Joey a blank look but not me! Uncle Randy has made sure I'm educated on these important beverage matters.

I leave and get their drinks ready at the server station, adding ice and red straws. I carefully balance the drinks on a tray and I walk back to their booth.

"How's the camp planning going?" I ask, setting the drinks down in front of the appropriate person.

"Good," David closes his menu, surprising us all by being the first one to comment on the question. "The songs are pretty catchy. Easy to learn too."

"And easy to chord along to," Mandy adds her menu to the stack.

Joey does the same. "A couple years ago, the songs were really lame but the program has definitely improved."

I take the stack of black menus, tucking them under my arm. I get out my notepad and pencil from my apron's front pocket. "What's the theme this year?"

"Love all around the world."

They tell me a bit more about their vision for the summer Bible camp. On average, thirty-five kids show up each day of the week. Throughout the day, kids travel from different stations, outdoor games, crafts, Bible story re-enactments where leaders bring to life well known stories in costume and then a music session with all the different age groups joining back together. Ages of kids are between five and twelve. The last day is set apart for teens, thirteen to eighteen. That day, more "teenage" things will be swapped in, like water fights, dodge ball, *Minute to Win It* games and a fear challenge. One challenge they've planned is teams being dared to eat melted Mars Bars out of diapers and digging for sliced hotdogs with their feet, in a vat of prepared oatmeal.

"Each day has a specific theme that all the games, Bible stories and crafts incorporate that day," David says, more talkative then I've ever seen him.

It must be the topic of kids and music that makes him more comfortable to share and comment. "What are some of the themes?" I ask, balancing my empty tray against my hip.

Mandy finishes dumping a sugar packet into her pop. I cringe. There is a ton of sugar in that already. "Love is the umbrella theme this year. On specific days, it's loving your family, loving your friends, loving strangers, and loving enemies." She reaches for another sugar packet. "There's another day but I can't remember the theme for Friday."

Joey is staring right at me and I shift uncomfortably. "The last theme is loving yourself," he says quietly.

"Oh," is all I say.

I take their orders after that. Beef dip and fries with extra gravy for Joey, personal Hawaiian pizza for David and fish and chips and tossed salad with ranch for Mandy. Extra tartar sauce.

I interact with the group easily in between their meal. We joke as I check in for refills, ask how everything is tasting and when I set the receipts on the table.

"Here's your bills. No rush, but I can take you at the front when you're ready," I tell them, my standard line when delivering receipts to tables. I've probably said it over five hundred times this summer.

"That would be simply lovely." Joey says in an impeccable British accent.

"Smashing indeed," Mandy says in a poor Indian accent, catching on quickly. Accents is her favourite game. We played it with a few other young adults during bowling. The rules are simple. You just keep carrying on your normal conversation but now with the addition of an accent. You have to choose an accent that hasn't already been claimed by someone else. Needless to say, British and American accents, the easier ones to mimic, are typically claimed first.

David pulls out bills from his pocket. "We can pay cash at the table." His Japanese accent is flawless, having spoken his native tongue at home all his life.

I only have one accent I can poorly manage that's still open for taking. "Well, laddie, that'll be just fine," Joey cringes at my Scottish accent attempt.

"Gold star for trying, Cara," he pulls out his wallet from his pocket. "How much do I owe?" His British accent is smooth, very convincing.

I take his receipt, smiling. "Nine-fifty," I say, finding the amount. "And don't laugh, you took the only accent I'm good at." My accent is definitely not close to accurate. More like a combination of Russian, Mexican and something else clearly not Scottish.

The group stands and Joey calls me closer with a single finger. He kisses my cheek when he feels me near. "I've missed you this week. Your laugh in person doesn't compare to a LOL over text."

I smile. "If you love me, next time leave the British accent for me."

He takes the arm David holds out. "But then I wouldn't get to laugh as much when we play Accents," he grins as they start to walk. "Until we meet again, love!" he calls over his shoulder, happily, still in English character.

I watch them go, David helping Joey through the busy lunch room. It's easier for someone to help Joey sometimes, especially with kids running around and chairs being unpredictably pushed out. And servers rushing around, with a one mind set of imputing orders into the system to send electronically to the kitchen. Mac sometimes comes to the restaurant but he's at the vet today for his yearly shots.

The sight of my friends helping Joey warms me. It reminds me of how beautiful it is to help others. And to allow yourself to be helped. *Not a weak thing but a sign of strength.* These words, from a truth statement recipe card of mine, remain with me the rest of the busy lunch hour.

Chapter 6

Before I know it, it's the weekend again. Saturday is spent rollerblading with Jack then flying kites with both him and Joey. Saturday evening, Mandy and David join us for a campfire and roasting marshmallows at Joey's, along with Erica and Isaac. Sunday morning comes early. We stayed up chatting around the fire until two am. But it's a tiredness that's worth it. The memory of the fun conversation and good company makes pulling myself from my warm bed easy.

Well, a bit easier.

The sermon today is based on the love chapter, 1 Corinthians. Joey's dad preaches on love being patient, and how that doesn't always mean the typical definition of patience. As usual, he's wearing a sharp looking suit. His white hair and wrinkles show his age of fifty-nine.

"The section on love being patient can also refer to being patient for finding it's partner. As in, being patient for the right timing. Sometimes lessons need to be learned separately before a couple should meet or pursue a relationship."

Hmm, I know a few girls who are desperate for boyfriends. It would do them good to hear that verse in a new light. I hang on to Pastor Harvey's words, vaguely aware of my uncle taking notes to my right and Jack doodling on the bulletin to my left.

"Another new way to look at this familiar passage is to insert the word *God* into each place the word *love* appears." Pastor Harvey reads the original passage: "Love is patient, love is kind. It does not envy, it does not boast, it is not proud. It does not dishonor others, it is not self-seeking, it is not easily angered, it keeps no record of wrongs. Love does not delight in evil but rejoices with the truth. It always protects, always trusts, always hopes, and always perseveres." He moves to the side of the pulpit, leaning on it. Next, he demonstrates his previously described method. "So you would say *God* is patient, *God* is kind, *God* does not keep record of wrongs and so forth." It certainly is a fresh take on a familiar verse.

After the service, I make my way over to Joey's family and say a quick hello. "Great sermon, Pastor Harvey," I say, shaking his hand. "I'll be pondering your new take on the love chapter for a while."

He can't stick around long, he's got to go greet people as they leave the front doors. But he does take my hand, brown eyes warm, crinkling at the corners. "Thanks, sweetheart. That's very kind." So are his ocean blue eyes. Joey and Erica favour their father as their mother, Savannah Waterloo, is blond.

I visit a few more minutes with Joey, his mom, Erica and Isaac. I notice Jack waving wildly at me and take it as my cue to leave. "Guess that's my exit sign."

Erica looks behind me. "Cutest exit sign I've ever seen." Isaac and Joey are chatting about where to eat for lunch so I don't have to explain the visual to Joey. "See you tonight, at the fair?" Her long dark curls are braided today, hanging to the side over her shoulder in a single braid. She reminds me of the striking dark haired beauty, Katniss, from the *Hunger Games* movies.

"Yup, I'll meet you guys there."

"Sounds good." She waves goodbye and then turn to listen in to the boy's conversation. Surprise, surprise, I hear Joey suggesting Subway.

After an easy lunch of tuna sandwiches and leftover potato salad from supper the night before, Jack and I start on our project.

Digging a hole to China.

Ever since I mentioned I tried unsuccessfully as a kid, he's wanted to try.

"Good luck," Aunt Jill calls out, looking up from her magazine when we pass by the back deck, plastic sand shovels in hand.

"Don't forget your manners when you meet the Chinese. Maybe look up how to say hello," is Uncle Randy's contributions to our send off. "All knowing Google should be able to help you out with that."

I roll my eyes but smile.

"I'm pretty sure you lacked an important part last time you tried to dig to China," Jack tells me when we get to the park.

I sit down next to him on the sand, near the playground center. "And what was that?"

He grins, digging his blue mini shovel into the sand. "Me!"

"Yup, that had to be it."

We giggle and laugh as we dig the afternoon away. When I stop to take a drink of water and check the time, I'm shocked it's four already. We've been here for two hours.

I peer into the hole.

China still is a lot of digging away.

"Maybe we should've tried Australia," Jack says, dirt and sweat covering his sunscreen laded face and arms.

After admiring our work, we tiredly sprawl out on the hot sand. We've both given up for today. "Why Australia?"

"Isn't its second name the down under? Maybe it means it would be easier to dig to."

"Oh, Jack," is all I can say as we gather our things and head on home. "You are the cutest cousin ever."

"Cute enough to get a piggy back ride?"

I hand him my shovel and then crouch down. He hops on and wraps his arms around my neck. Rising, I carry him home. He hums "It's a Small World" the entire way home. By the time I walk up the driveway, my shoulders are aching. I remember him being a lot lighter last time I gave him a piggy back. Granted, that was probably a few years back.

"Thank you for getting that annoying song stuck in my head, Jack," I say as he hops down. "I now feel like I'm on Splash Mountain at Disneyland."

"You are welcome, Cara. Disneyland is the happiest place on earth." Our laughter trails us into the house. *An afternoon well spent, even if we didn't get to China.* And tonight has the potential to be just as fun.

***

Seven rolls around quickly and even though the early shift is mine tomorrow morning, I'm full of energy for another evening out. I pull my car into the mall parking lot, across the highway from the East Side Café. The travelling amusement park is set up in the parking lot. Crowds of families mingle about the various game booths. I join them, marvelling at the excitement around me. The smell of cotton candy, popcorn and cinnamon sugared mini doughnuts fills the air.

I find the others near the dunk tank.

"Hey!" Isaac spots me first. "We were just debating whether to call you."

Late is not my style. I got caught up talking to Jack about what superhero would make a better brother just as I was about to leave. A conversation I don't regret. "Sorry. I would say I got caught behind the train but that's on the other side of town."

Joey loops his arm around my neck playfully. "Tried that line myself back in high school. It would've worked if my buddy, Mike, didn't blurt out to the teacher where I lived. Totally opposite side of town from the train tracks."

We all laugh, none of us doubting Joey trying a stunt like that.

"What should we do first?" Erica asks, looking around at all the options. "Ferris wheel? That strawberry ride that twirls you around?"

Isaac points to the cotton candy stand. "Let's save the ferris wheel for last, it's my favourite."

The group heads over to the food booths. Even though I had supper before, the smells tempt me.

We purchase our snacks and head to a table. The conversations around are lively. Seas of excited kids and adults talk about the rides, the ones they've been on and the ones they still want to try. I'm glad Aunt Jill is bringing Jack and a friend here tomorrow afternoon.

"Maybe this was a bad decision," Erica says, licking the dripping ketchup from the side of her corndog. "I don't want to find out how this tastes regurgitated."

"Most likely like barf," Joey says, as usual no filter in place around his sister. "But ketchup flavoured barf."

"Eww!" She wrinkles her nose and then pushes the last half of her corn dog in Isaac's direction. He gladly begins chomping on it, his own corndog finished in three bites.

I excuse myself and find the row of blue porta potties. I head straight to the portable sink to the side and wash my hands, getting rid of the sticky feeling left over from the blue and pink cotton candy I shared with Joey.

The evening flies by. Thankfully, no one's food comes back up and we all enjoy the rides and game booths. Isaac wins a stuffed unicorn for Erica at a dart throwing booth. Joey wins me a monkey from a ring toss both.

Erica and I hold our prizes fondly as we stand in line for the last ride of the evening, the ferris wheel.

"I'm glad we saved this for later in the evening," I comment, looking up at the giant wheel. Night is fast approaching and the dark sky gives a striking backdrop to the white lights wound all around the chairs of the ride. I bet my family can see the lit structure from our house.

We hand the operator our tickets and get on. Isaac and Erica are in one chair and Joey and I are in the following one.

My stomach lurches as we start to move. "I haven't been on one of these forever."

He takes my hand. "I was on this one last year, but definitely not with as beautiful company."

"Who were you with?"

"Isaac."

"Nice." We are quiet and I'm enjoying the feel of the breeze in my hair and my skin. I debate describing the view to Joey but then decide against it. Instead, I close my eyes and try to experience the ride as he is. The subtle movement of the ride intensifies when my sight is gone. I notice a gently rocking of the chair that I didn't before. It's repetitive rhythm is comforting, like a mother cradling her child to sleep.

"My dad's sermon on 1 Corinthians got me thinking today," Joeys shares quietly. I open my eyes. We are stopped at the top of the ride, new people being allowed onto empty chairs at the bottom of the ride. I know Joey often offers advice to his dad when he's preparing his sermon. But he has new revelations about the sermon when he hears the finished product on Sunday mornings with the rest of the congregation.

"Me too. It was really powerful."

"Agreed." The breeze plays in his dark hair and I resist the urge to do the same with my fingers. I don't want to distract him from his sharing. "You know how he said to change the word *love* to *God* every time in the verse? What if we exchanged the word *love* for our names?"

It takes a moment but then I understand. "As in is *Cara* is patient, is *Cara* is kind?"

"Exactly. To serve as a checklist, to see if we are living our lives like God would, like a loving person would."

"Wow, that's an awesome way to look at it." The ride begins moving again. We don't say much the rest of the ride. I keep musing over what Joey said and he's lost in thought himself. I don't mind. I love how we can go for long periods of time just thinking about life beside each other, enjoying each other's presence but praying or thinking on our own.

"Thanks for the ride," Joey tells the operator when he lifts the bar of our chair, letting us off.

The man tips his baseball cap in acknowledgment. I recognize him as a worker at the grocery store, in the meat shop section.

I look around. The crowds are thinning. Most of the rides are shutting down. There's a trail of people walking to their cars, happy expressions on all. "Where are Erica and Isaac? I thought they got on before us."

Joey opens his mouth to answer but a shriek interrupts him.

I whip around to find Erica running towards me. "He did it! He did it!" she holds out her left hand, a sparkly ring in place. "Right on top of the ferris wheel!"

Eyes wide, heart surprised, I take her hand and admire the silver ring. A light from the ferris wheel behind me catches the ring, casting a line of sparkles on the ground. "What a place to propose!"

Joey clamps a hand on Isaac. Even with the dark sky and his dark skin, I can tell Isaac's grinning.

Big.

"Nicely done, my future brother in law," Joey admired. "Way to set the bar high."

I look up from admiring the ring. He's looking in my direction. It's way too soon to be talking weddings, when we don't even live in the same town the majority of the year. When our dating is still new. When we haven't known each other two months yet.

Then just try to wipe that stupid grin off your face, Cara. Or try to tell that blush to stop. And those butterflies fluttering in your stomach? Definitely not stopping any time soon with that boy looking at you like that.

The walk to our cars is spent talking about Isaac's nerves beforehand, how Erica almost ruined his plan of proposing romantically at night when the ride was lit up, when she suggested doing it first. Then Erica starts dreaming about white dresses, caterers and the best season for pictures to get married in.

She's giddy. Not very Katniss like.

I grin.

I happen to think a woman in love is adorable. Ironically, this stage of adulthood brings out the little girl inside of her.

And one look to my side, where Joey is leaned up against my car, listening to his sister gush, tells me I'm not the only one. The look on his face says he thinks a woman in love is just as entertaining. And a thing he longs and prays for.

And so that night I do just that. I pray that one day God will bring an Isaac into my life to cherish, teach and challenge me. But someone that I support and love back. I fall asleep with a smile on my face, certain God hears me and hoping that one day He answers my prayers. That one day I get to wear the same expression, that Erica likely wore stepping off the ferris wheel. The one I saw when she excitedly showed off her ring.

The expression of being head over heels in love, from a match made in heaven.

Chapter 7

"Really? *This* is the activity you came up with? For me to experience being blind doing?"

I am not impressed. Not over being blindfolded for an hour but over the prospect of getting wet. As in drenched. Bathing Mac will no doubt do that to me.

"Come on, it'll be fun," Joey ties the folded red bandanna over my eyes.

I hear Mandy and David snicker.

"If any one of you tapes this, it's friends off." I grit my teeth. I'm feeling irritated today and have been all day at work. I think it's from being scheduled to work with the rail thin, bulimic waitress, Laura. It's so hard to not compare how my body looks next to hers. I'm a giant next to her.

Cara, are you being patient with your friends? How about kind? Easily angered? I hold in a heavy sigh. Definitely not living up to the love chapter checklist. *Or what about Laura? Maybe you should ask her if she wants to talk.* The thought makes me cringe. I don't like sharing my story. But I do like being friends with the people with me right now. So I try again, this time in a kinder voice. It was my idea to "try out" blindness after all. "What I mean is, can we please try not to get me soaked?"

"No guarantees but we can try," Joey says and I hear the sound of water running. I picture him filling the plastic blue kid pool with the garden house. We're in his backyard and I'm sure it'll be a Saturday afternoon I won't forget.

At least it's sunny out so I'll dry fast. And it's only water. And I'm in good company, I tell myself, trying to snap out of my funk and keep looking at the positives. *My grumpy mood and bad emotions won't last. And a cheerful heart and attitude can go a long way to help.*

"Okay, here we go," Mandy takes my hand and leads me to the pool. I don't like being at the mercy of someone else. My steps are timid and slow.

Someone touches my shoulder. "You okay?" I hear Joey ask.

"Fine, "I say, lying.

"Liar," I hear the smile in his voice. "You're hating every minute of this."

I ignore him and focus on the task instead. "Are we at the pool yet?"

"Almost. About three feet left to go,"

My foot bumps into the pool. Joey must have kept filling it a bit after I was blindfolded. It wasn't full enough to splash water out before. My wet runners say it is now.

A whistle from my right. "Mac! Here, buddy!"

I hear the bell on Mac's collar jingle and then feel something furry breeze past the bare calf peeking out from my rolled up jeans. I'm thinking my pink tank top and pony tail were wise choices. I've seen Mac playing in the water before. That dog loves swimming the way kids love ice cream.

Someone hands me a bottle. I assume it's shampoo.

"Soap," David's voice explains, on my left.

I feel so lost without my sight. Unbalanced. Like I'm in one of my power yoga classes standing in tree pose, trying to stay steading on one foot, arms raised.

A familiar hand takes my free one. "First step is to kneel down, to Mac's height." I follow Joey's instruction and lower myself to my knees. My hands find the rim of the pool. I stick my hand into the cool water. "Is Mac in yet?" A splash surprises me, causing me to drop the soap bottle. "Ahh!"

Multiple laughs. I easily distinguish which one belongs to who. "He is now," Mandy's voice comes from above me. She must be behind me, standing over me.

A strange textured object is handed to me. It takes me a second to identify it. A sponge.

"Dip it in the water then pour some soap on it," Joey says, the expert in washing his golden retriever.

I do as he says. "Mac, get over here," I say, not sure where to face. The pool is big. Mac could be way on the other side. A wet nose touches my empty hand, locating the dog. "Hey, Mac," I say, working the soapy sponge into his fur.

A lick to my nose.

"Careful, he might take advantage of you," I hear Joey say, surprising me. He must be kneeling beside me now. I didn't even feel him lower down. "He might try to kiss you."

I open my mouth to respond but Mac intervenes. With a big sloppy wet kiss. "Bleh!" I jump back, the sponge flying away from me. I hear it splash into the pool.

Heavy breathing and splashing follow. I picture Mac chasing his tail, playing in the water.

My friends are laughing behind me.

Determined, I crawl on all fours back to the pool. Reaching in, I fish around for the sponge. I can't find it. *Ah, what does it matter now? I've just inhaled dog food breath and I'm already wet.* Two seconds later, I'm in the middle of the pool, seated on my knees.

"Did she just...?"

"Didn't know she had it in her," Mandy says, surprise in her voice. "Joey, your girlfriend totally just climbed into the pool."

"She's a feisty one, my girl." I smile, imagining Joey's proud look. Usually spontaneous acts are his forte.

"Mac, you stink," I say into the air, not caring anymore how I look if I'm facing the opposite direction of the dog. "You need a bath. Get your furry self over here. *Now.*"

Trained to pick up different tones in voices, Mac senses my frustration and determination. A wet paw touches my knee. "Good boy," I say and then continue to work the soap into this fur.

"Looks good," David encourages, watching with the others.

Next step is to rinse him off. I don't ask for help but crawl clumsily out of the pool. Knowing I look like a zombie with my outstretched arms, I move into the direction of house.

"Whoa! Where ya going?" Mandy's suddenly at my side.

"To get the hose."

"It's on the ground, by the pool."

Oh, right. I forget they had used it fill the pool. "Well that saves me a trip."

I turn around and head back in the direction I came.

A throat clears. "Change your course fifteen degrees, friend."

"Thanks, David," I shift my path slightly and find the pool. Dropping to all fours, I search around until I find the hose. Finding the trigger on the sprayer, I aim it in the direction of the pool.

Then I stop.

A slow smile.

I change the direction of my aim. Then push down on the trigger.

"Ahhh!"

"Crazy girlfriend!"

"She's armed!"

I stand to my feet and pull off the bandanna, able to aim the spray of cold water more efficiently now. "That's right and she's relentless. No mercy for you!"

Mandy and David run towards the watering cans. They start filling them up with the rain barrel by the side of the house. *But where's Joey?*

Arms wrap around my waist. I shriek in surprise.

"You feel way too dry, Cara," Joey says. He tugs me towards the pool. "Care for a dip?"

"Don't you dare!" I laugh, squirming in his hold. But his arms are stronger than mine. He throws me into the pool with a splash. Mandy and David show up just then and dump their watering cans over my head.

"Joey, we got her with watering cans, your turn."

Joey takes his cue from Mandy and squeezes the soapy sponge over my head. "Good teamwork, guys," he says, making sure he gets every single drop out before tossing it aside.

I spit out a mouthful of water. "And I thought *Mac* was going to get me wet today."

Joey dips his hand in the pool and splashes me. And apparently it's time for Accents again, his next words coming out in an impeccable German accent. "You're the one who initiated it, yah? Point a finger at us and four are pointed back at you, Cara."

I lift my hand from the water and point a finger. Then I realize some of my fingers *are* actually pointing back at me. I laugh, my answer in a pretty decent British accent. "I have nothing to say in my defence."

Mac wanders over and nudges Joey's leg with his nose. He must have jumped out of the pool when he saw Joey pulling me towards the pool. Joey reaches down and pets his head. "Did you notice I saved the British accent for you this time?"

"I did, thank you."

"Remember what you said that would mean?"

I search my mind as I climb out of the pool. I vaguely remember having this conversation the day we last played Accents. I think it was when they were at the restaurant. "Remind me again?" I take the towel Mandy offers me and start to dry my hair, squeezing out the water.

Mandy gives David a towel and then starts winding up the hose. David leaves to return the water cans.

"Are they gone?" Joey asks.

"Yeah, why?"

Suddenly, he's very near my face. "You said if I loved you I would save the British accent for you."

Ah, yes, now I remember. "Aww, what a sweet boyfriend you are."

"Not that sweet." A gleam in his eye.

I give him a funny look he can't see. "No, you're pretty swee-"

Arms snake around my waist, locking me in place. My soaked tank top is stretched from the water, much longer then it was an hour ago. I realize a second to late what Joey's planning and try to get free. But again his arms are stronger. Tickles to my side come before I can protest and call for help. Better late than never though. "Stop, you positively evil boyfriend!" I cry out.

"Not until you say you love me!"

He tickles near my rib and I lean away from it, laughing. It feels like I hit a funny bone. Unpleasant but it makes me giggle. I don't want to give in so easy but tickles are my weakness. Tickle me in the feet any day but try my side and I'm reduced to a wimp. "Fine, fine! I love you!" Tears are streaming from my face, not from pain but laughter.

Joey wraps his arms around me, tenderly now. "Love you too, Cara. Every water drenched part of you."

We don't kiss but the moment feels like the ones that prelude to a kiss.

"Want to go get some food?" Mandy interrupts, David following close behind. Her eyes widen, realizing what she's stumbled into. "Oh, uh, sorry, didn't mean to intrude."

Joey shrugs, dropping his arms to his side. The front of his shirt has a wet spot where I was pressed against him. "I have plenty of years to kiss her."

"Aww, you guys are adorable!" Mandy lets her long bond dreads lose from her pony tail. "Make sure to give me an invite to wedding. I want to share this story at open mic."

The group laughs and we move inside to dry off. Thankfully, I brought a set of dry clothes. The others aren't as wet as me and don't need to change. Once I'm in dry shorts and a t-shirt, curls air-drying, we decide to go pick up sushi at the grocery store.

"And some veggies and dip," Mandy requests as we are discussing our early supper. It's four in the afternoon.

"And some ice cream sandwiches," Joey adds. I'm learning that along with Subway, this boy adores ice cream. His favourite is vanilla sundaes covered in sprinkles and caramel sauce. Add on some chocolate sauce and smarties and he looks like a newly crowned king seated on a throne. I can't count how many times I've asked him what he is doing, over text or phone, and the answer is simply "Eating ice cream, what else would I be doing?"

Needless to say, I've acquired a love of ice cream sundaes myself. I like to think Joey's company is my favourite topping, the one that I can't resist each time he suggests a sundae making date night.

We walk to the store, about twenty minutes from Joey's. We're all hesitant to leave the air conditioned building but then find some shade in a nearby park. Sitting on the grass, we spread out our picnic supper.

"Mmm, California rolls are my favourite." I pick up one of the rice rolled packages. Seconds later, avocado, cucumber, carrot and crab delightfully fill my mouth.

"Nah, the Dynamite ones are the best. The flying fish sauce is so good. Sounds gross though."

Intrigued by my boyfriend's review, I try one and agree. "I don't think I've ever had that kind before. I usually stick to California rolls."

David expertly handles his chopsticks. Joey is doing the same but Mandy and I have left ours in the plastic packages. Mandy declared she would starve if she had to use them. I use a fork but Mandy decided to go "cave man style" and use her hands. That girl is so funny. Such a compliment to David's quiet nature.

"You never know what you're missing until you give it a chance. You just might love it." Joey comments then asks where the vegetables are. I fill his plate with an assortment of them, indicating which one is where, using the position of a clock for a visual. I don't always but we have a secret indication that he uses when he would like to know. A tug to the ear. I saw it today so I quietly told him.

"Hey, speaking of love, that reminds me," David wipes his mouth with a napkin. He polished off his twelve sushi rolls in five minutes. From the way he's eyeing the raw vegetables, I take it the next thing he'll be eating is the ice cream sandwiches. "You were going to ask her to speak at camp, Joey."

"Oh, right, totally forgot." Joey sets his paper plate on his lap and turns to me. "As a team, we decided a guest speaker might be a powerful way to illustrate some of the themes."

"And you want me to be the guest speaker?"

"Yeah, on the last day, when the theme is about loving yourself."

My eyes shift to Mandy and David. They don't know about my eating disorder days. "Why me?" I hope Joey didn't confide in them about my past. It wasn't his story to share.

"I thought of you, actually," David says. He's getting more talkative the more I hang out with him and Mandy. "You have a way with words and I just thought you might have a creative way to illustrate loving yourself."

Relieved that Joey didn't break my confidence, I nod. But then I shake my head. "I actually hate public speaking." I tell them about fainting once in high school and then breaking out into hives from the stress of oral presentations during university. "I'm honored by the request, but I think I have to pass."

Disappointment shows on Joey's face. He knows better than Mandy and David how well my life fits with that theme. But to be honest, I still don't feel like an expert on the topic. I still struggle. I would feel like a hypocrite standing up there talking to kids and teens about loving yourself when I have a hard time doing that myself. It's still a mountain I have to climb, a giant I have to conquer. Public speaking isn't my favorite thing to do. But even if it were, I don't think I'd agree to tell my story. Not when healing is still in progress.

David looks sad too. "That's unfortunate. I had a really good feeling you would say yes. I thought maybe God placed you on my heart for a reason." A shrug. "Guess not."

This has happened before. When God clearly has wanted me to do something but it scares me. Sometimes, I'm obedient to the leading and other times I rebel. I'm choosing to rebel this time, even though my mind is picturing countless times where I was obedient and each time I never regretted it. Good things resulted, even if I didn`t see it at first. Things like strangers encouraged by a compliment or doors opening from taking a risk.

"We can ask someone else," Mandy tells me, noting the boy's disappointment. "Obviously God has someone else in mind to speak to the camp on the Friday."

I can't say I don't enjoy the rest of the day with my friends but I do feel different after that conversation. Like there is someone nudging me, in a direction I don't want to go.

Fine, God, I tell Him after I finish washing my face and brushing my teeth that night. I pad down the hallway and climb into bed. *I'll do it if You give me a creative way to illustrate loving yourself. The one I clearly don't have in my possession now. The one David thought I would have.*

I don't get an audible response, but a verse from a sermon a few weeks comes to mind. I think it is from Luke, maybe chapter eleven or twelve. The Bible is a way God often communicates to me. And tonight's His voice rings loud and clear through the verse:

The right words will be there. The Holy Spirit will give you the right words when the time comes.

***

It's August before I come to a startling conclusion: Joey and I have never actually had an official date night. Like the dress up and go out for dinner kind.

"Pick you up at seven? And wear a dress," is Joey's response when I bring it up over the phone one afternoon. I'm lying on my back on my bed, still in my black dress clothes from work. I look at the clock on the side table, it's just after five. I texted Joey when I got home around three, saying a nap was needed instead of our planned afternoon ice cream run to Dairy Queen.

We've been able to see more of each other lately. His seminary assignments slowed down a few weeks back. And I'm back to the morning shifts, which I prefer. I'm tired after a steady eight hours of waitressing. I don't know how Joey handle's distance classes and work. But I guess his job does allow him more flexible hours. And some of his work at the church acts as research for his classes.

Joey says he'll take care of reservations and then has to leave, a counselling client has arrived. He may be the music pastor but his duties are far from only music things some days. He says lyrics from songs often come to mind for him, to encourage clients with or to pray over them at the end of sessions.

"Sometimes my prayers sound really deep and eloquent," he told me once when we were walking Mac, hand in hand. "But I'm really just reciting well-loved lyrics."

"God uses it either way, to uplift people."

The memory fades and my closet comes into view. *What to wear, what to wear?* I bite the side of my lip softly, in the middle of a typical woman's life dilemma: a closet full but nothing to wear.

After I model three dresses, getting Aunt Jill and Jack's opinion as they do a word search together at the kitchen table, I finally decide on a dark purple dress. I actually haven't worn it yet, the price tag still dangles under the armpit. I slip it on and admire the fit of the empire waist dress in my full length mirror.

Soft stylish ruffles run down from the strapless neckline, ending at the empire waist. I turn around, the rich colored material swishing at my legs. It's noticeably longer at the back, a look I once found strange but have grown to like.

I add some pearl earrings, refresh my makeup, apply some red lipstick, a silver bangle and turn my wild curls into more tame ringlets with a curling iron. Now I'm ready to go.

When I enter the kitchen, black clutch in hand, Uncle Randy is just getting home from work. A low whistle as he takes my appearance in. "Someone's getting a very pretty date tonight," he says, setting a stack of papers down on the island.

"Is it okay?" I ask, looking down at the dress. "I'm so used to wearing black dresses at work that this color feels extremely outgoing."

"It's lovely, Cara."

"Yeah!" Jack agrees, waving his pencil in the air, looking up from his word search. "You look like a sugar plum fairy."

Uncle Randy grabs an apple from the basket on the center of the island. "Are those fairies actually purple in *The Nutcracker,* Jack?"

He thinks about it, making the cutest face. His blond curls are as wild as ever and his blue eyes look troubled as he tries to recall the ballet our families went to together four Christmases ago. "Now that you mention it, I don't know. But plums are purple and so was that cabbage Mom put in the coleslaw yesterday." He shrugs his small shoulders. "I guess to be safe, I should just say you look like a cabbage fairy, Cara."

My nerves still tingle in my stomach but I laugh. Even though I know Joey won't be able to see the dress, I still want to feel confident and beautiful in it. "Thanks, Jack. You always know what to say to make me laugh."

"It's what I'm here for," he mumbles, attention back on the word search.

I walk over to the table, my heels clicking against the tiles. After pressing a quick kiss to the top his curls, I wave to my aunt and uncle and then head out.

I gasp when I see what's in the driveway.

A white limo. With Joey leaning against the side, suit jacket swung over the shoulder of a blue dress shirt. A black, white and navy striped tie, black dress pants and shiny black shoes accentuate the look.

"You really went all out," I say, still in shock. The stretched car takes up nearly the entire driveway.

He holds out his arm for me and I take it, looping my arm through it. "First official dates are meant to be done in style."

"You certainly nailed that." I take in his clothes, his gorgeous blue eyes and slightly ruffled dark hair from the breeze. "And you are looking pretty stylish yourself tonight."

A shrug. "I try."

I nudge him playfully in the side and then he opens the door. "Ladies first."

Feeling like I'm Cinderella entering the pumpkin carriage on her way to a ball, I giggle and duck my head in. Joey closes the door behind me and reappears a few seconds later, entering from the opposite side of the car.

"To The Collsseum," he tells our driver. The man nods and puts the car in reverse, slowly backing out of the driveway onto the street.

Joey takes my hand. "I should've said this the second I heard you close the front door." A kind smile, his eyes alive with excitement for an elegant evening together. "You look absolutely stunning tonight, Cara."

"Thanks," I accept the compliment. "Even if you have no idea it's true. I could be wearing sweats for all you know."

"Are you?"

I smile. "No."

"Didn't think so."

"Don't you want to know what I'm wearing? Want me to describe my dress to you, like I do the stars or the sunsets?"

He thinks about it but then shakes his head. "Not that I don't think the dress looks as nice as those things but I only need to know one thing about it."

The color? The style? The length? I don't have a good guess what he'll ask. "And that would be?"

He raises an eyebrow, pinning me with a look I can only describe as dead serious. "Do you feel beautiful in it?"

I cast a glance down at the rich plum colored material spilling out before me over the black leather interior of the seats. I really don't have to think about it. "Yes, I do."

He leans back against the seat and closes his eyes. "Then that's all I need to know."

The driver turns on some soft jazz music. I close my eyes and lean against the headrest, letting the piano music wash over me. It's not as beautiful as listening to Joey play, maybe because it lacks the visual of someone swaying to created music, eyes closed, passion for the instrument evident. But the pianist on the stereo does create a romantic mood.

When we pull up to the restaurant, Joey gets out and beats the driver to opening my door. "May I assist you to your table?" he asks, grinning. I honestly think he wears a smile more than anyone I know. The most worn item of his, by a landslide.

"You may," I take his arm and step out of the limo. Then it's my turn to lead. With arms looped, we slowly make our way to the front door of one of the fancier restaurants in town. East Side Café is more of a family restaurant but The Colosseum is usually where older couples or wedding parties reserve. *Or boyfriends wanting to impress their girlfriend on a first date.*

The evening is straight from something playing at the theaters. From appetizers of crab legs, plated with beautiful garnishes that I immediately snap pictures of on my phone, to our main meal of the chef's special of white wine chicken stew over wild rice, it's the richest and delectable meal I've tasted.

Though I've only eaten half of the serving on my plate, I agree to share dessert.

"How can we not?" Joey tells the server when he questions us about bringing the dessert menu. "But I think we already know what we want." He looks at me. "The raspberry white chocolate cheesecake, right?"

I nod. "You know it." Erica and Isaac have been raving about the decadent dessert for weeks, ever since they came here after getting engaged.

When the dessert arrives, I gasp. "Joey! This cheesecake could serve four people!"

He finds his fork. "Not to fear, I know for a fact leftover cheesecake does not lose its quality or enjoyment value."

"Well, that's a relief."

"Isn't it, though?"

We grin at each other and then dig in. I moan when the first bite passes through my lips. "I think I know my answer now."

Joey looks surprised, as if he didn't actually believe his sister's description of the dessert living up to the hype. "What question was I asking?" He breaks off a piece of the thick white dessert, rolling the piece in the chocolate and raspberry sauce swirls decorating the plate underneath.

I finish my bite, a full fresh raspberry and white chocolate chip in that piece. There are milk chocolate chips spread throughout the dessert as well. "The question of what you would want to survive on, if you were shipwrecked on a deserted island and you could only pick one food to have in limitless supply."

Understanding dawns. "Ah, yes, nice choice."

"What would you pick?"

"Ice cream."

"Right, dumb question."

"Just shows your memory is going." He sets his fork down and wipes his face with his red cloth napkin before laying it on the table. "Just imagine what you'll be like when we're old and grey, if your memory is fading already at twenty-one."

I kick him in the shin gently. "Watch it, buddy. You're the older one. You'll be admitted to the senior's home before me."

"Only if they serve ice cream regularly for dessert."

We talk about everything and yet nothing at all. My birthday last week celebrated with friends and family at a BBQ my aunt and uncle hosted, about Joey's classes, his sister's excitement for the wedding and how we should start doing more Sudoku to exercise our fading memories. There is one topic we avoid though. The one we've been tip toeing around for most of the summer.

The summer ending. As in, me leaving back to the city for nine months. And who knows where I will be the next summer? I might end up staying in the city, working at a job that allows me to work with kids, something to add to my resume for when I'm done with my education degree and looking for a teaching job. I hope it doesn't come up tonight, ruining the evening with sadness.

"Don't be mad but I did something maybe I shouldn't have."

I frown at Joey, wishing sometimes my expressions were effective. But tone of voice is a second best. "Go on."

He detects the start of distrust and rushes on. "We still haven't filled the guest speaker position, for the loving yourself theme day for camp."

My stomach tightens. God hasn't given me the creative idea I bargained with Him for yet. That doesn't mean the nudging and sense of being disobedient for not agreeing hasn't let up yet though. I try to shove the thought away but it's difficult given Joey is still engaging me in a conversation about that uncomfortable topic. "And this has to do with me why? I already declined."

He looks uncomfortable. And guilty. Two expressions unfamiliar to his face. "I told David and Mandy a little about your past. About how you struggled with an eating disorder but are healed now, struggling sometimes still but starting to love yourself more, the way you are right now."

Betrayal claws all over me, like an army of hairy legged spiders. My mouth opens. I try to speak. No words come. At least not verbally. *I can't believe he did that! Spilled my personal story to our friends.*

Knowing what he did was wrong, he reaches for my hand. He barely touches it when I jerk away. "That wasn't your story to share," I say, coldly, a chill settling over our table. Over the evening.

There's a tug-a-war in his eyes. Like he regrets it but still agrees with the reasoning for sharing. "I realize that now. I really am sorry, Cara."

"Your eyes say differently." I fold my arms across my front. The cheesecake in my stomach suddenly feels like a lump of fat. I desperately wish I hadn't eaten it. Then maybe this moment wouldn't be effecting me. Then I would have a power over myself, some control to this horrible emotion of disappointment.

So he has flaws, the voice of reasons murmurs to me, even though I don't want to hear it. *All summer, love blinded you. You put him on a pedestal. People do unwise things and the wise thing is to forgive.*

"Look, can I please explain?" He pleads, desperation in his eyes. He can sense I'm seconds from bolting.

"What is there to explain? You went and publicly declared my past to our friends. Every time they look at me, they probably see the girl who is still ridiculously self-absorbed and worried about her looks." I'm on a tangent, anger spilling from the betrayed parts of me. "Mandy and David probably think I'm incredibly vain." I've gained the attention of a few tables and I lower my voice. "Weren't you listening to your dad that one Sunday? Love doesn't delight in evil."

Anger flashes in his eyes. "Might I remind you, it also says love is patient. As in please cool down, set your bruised ego aside for a minute and please listen to my explanation."

Bruised ego? "You are just digging yourself deeper into a-"

"Cara! I'm serious, just give me a second to explain."

I eye the exit door. Curiosity is the only thing that keeps me seated, though hurt is trying to yank me away. "Fine, explain." I glare at him, wishing he could see it.

He shifts uncomfortably and I hope he can feel the seething look I'm pinning him with. "I told them about your past so they would know why I agreed so strongly with David that you were the best candidate for the Friday guest speaker spot. So they could intensify their prayers for you to agree." He tries to reach for my hand but they are still angrily pinned against myself. Realizing my hands are not available, he leans back in his seat. "Cara, I didn't do it to defame you. I did it so you could have some specific extra prayer. To help work on your heart and be open to sharing. Your story is a powerful one, showing how God can free people."

I hear some of what he's saying but my fury is distracting. "They probably think I'm so stupid."

He blinks in surprise. "Mandy said she wished she knew, that you were more open about talking about it. Both David and I were surprised when she said she used to be Bulimic."

My anger dims a bit. Like someone tossed a bucket of water on the flames raging inside. Likely to return once the water sizzles out. "Oh."

"It was wrong to go behind your back. I should have asked."

"Yes, you should've, Joey."

"But do you see why I did it? Even Mandy could benefit from talking with you. We try to hide our brokenness from others but there is such strength and healing when we reveal it to others. To support each other. And mark my words, *everyone* has a brokenness they struggle with. Large or small, it's there."

I sigh, something I didn't image myself doing tonight. At least not the weary sighing. "I understand why you did it, Joey. And yes, God is knocking on the door of my heart. I think He wants me to speak that day but I'm being stubborn." I rise from my seat. "Thanks for dinner, it was delicious. But I need to go."

"Wait, Cara," he reaches out and grabs my arm. "Please don't leave. The evening can't end like this."

I gently pry his desperate hold off me. "It's not a happy ending like we both would've wanted but I'm not in the mood anymore. Don't worry about me, I'll just walk home."

Again he grabs my arm, stopping me. "You told me about your struggles, past and present, pretty much the first week we met.

"That was different. It was *my* choice to do that. And I felt strangely comfortable around you, even if you were a stranger." I'm pulling away, physically and emotionally. "I need to go, Joey. I can't be around you right now."

His look is pure torture. "I'm *so* sorry, Cara."

"You said that already." I wiggle out of his grasp. "Your heart was in the right place." I understand his reasoning, how my triumph story and even current struggles with body image could help others. But it doesn't erase the fact that he weakened my trust in him. Broken confidence is a tricky thing to strengthen. It takes time. "But you don't hurt someone else in the name of helping others."

Deep guilt and regret fills his eyes and he reaches for me again, trying to stall the inevitable. An evening ending in a fight.

"Don't touch me," I snap, the flames roaring back to life. Inside, I'm a wreck, sparks surging through my veins. Betrayal. Lack of control. Regret over the cheesecake. Disappointment. But most of all, terror. Of realizing Joey is right, we are all flawed.

I take my clutch from the table and leave. I don't look back, knowing his expression will kill me. I know he's genuinely sorry but I need space. Waves of sorrow fill me, overlapping the sandy beach line of betrayal. *He planned a dream date and I choose to end it like this.* But he was the one who'd gone behind me and spilled my secrets, good intentions or not. *Sometimes that's his flaw, getting so caught up in helping others that he unintentionally hurts others in his path.*

I get home thirty minutes later, barefooted, heels dangling from my hands. I'm tired, bloated, cold and angry. Tossing my heels in the front closet, I set my cutch down on the island. The walk home was dark and scary but I'm glad I didn't call home for a ride. I needed time to let my emotions settle. To cool off.

I look around. *Where is everyone?*

Deciding they must have went to take Jack to the park or to rent a movie, I open my clutch and dig around for my phone. My mom always gives the best advice. The kind that sometimes you don't want to hear but need to. She could shine some light on my dark situation.

I turn my phone on and frown. There are eight missed calls, within the course of the last hour and a half. From the same number. Aunt Jill. I check my text messages. There is only one.

"Call ASAP! @ the immergency room. Accident." The spelling errors alone are alarming. Aunt Jill's texts never include spelling mistakes or abbreviations. She's a firm believer in spelling words fully out and proofreading.

I phone her back and as it rings, my anger's replaced with fear. *What happened while I was gone? Who's hurt? Are they okay?*

She picks up on the fourth ring, sounding antsy. "Hello? "

"Aunt Jill! What's going on? Who's hurt?"

She sounds like she's been crying. "It's Jack. He..." her words turn to sobs and my heart breaks for her.

"Stay on the phone," I say, grabbing my keys from the basket by the front door. "I'm on the way."

Even though it's illegal in our province to be on the phone while driving, I press my phone to my ear and get into my car and peel out from the curb. I keep reassuring Aunt Jill with,

"It's okay," and "I'll be there soon". I have no idea if the first reassurance is true but I know at the speed I'm going the second one definitely is.

Aunt Jill doesn't say much but I gather from incoherent comments that Uncle Randy is hurt too. My foot presses harder against the gas. No one should be alone when loved ones are hurt. I push aside images of blood and torn limbs, focusing on a single goal of getting to Aunt Jill.

Once I'm at the hospital, I park crookedly in between two parking lanes and then run inside. Cool air condition blasts onto my bare shoulders when I enter through the automatic doors.

I look around, frantic. I hadn't got to this part of the plan yet. I've never been to the hospital before and am disoriented.

"Cara."

I spin around and find Aunt Jill. Rushing over, I drop down in front of her. Black streaks of mascara trail down her face. "What happened? Talk to me, Aunt Jill. Where's Uncle Randy?" I take a breath, trying to reign in my wild emotions. *One question at a time. She's still in a state of shock.* From the feel of my wide eyes, shaking arms, and the way I'm tightly gripping the tops of her thighs, I realize I probably am in shock too.

"There was an accident," Aunt Jill sniffs, hanging her head.

"Who?"

"Jack and Randy."

"Are they okay?" she shakes her head and I will my dinner to stay down. As nausea takes over, it threatens to spill out of my mouth. My head spins and my hands feel clammy against her white capris.

She doesn't answer but slowly lifts her head to meet my desperate gaze. I've never seen such a wounded and fearful look in another human's eyes. At least, aside from on a TV drama. Unfortunately this was my reality, my family being thrown into the tidal wave of pain. "Randy is getting stiches. He broke his arm."

A Filipino nurse walks by and stops beside us. "Mrs. Phelps? Can I have a word with you?"

I want to scream at her, demand that she leave us be. Aunt Jill still hasn't told me where Jack is. I need to know where that angel of a kid is. My worst nightmare suddenly births itself in my mind. *What if he's dead?"* I try to slam the brakes on my morbid way of thinking but it's too late.

I grab my aunt's shoulder, pushing aside the young nurse. "Where is Jack?"

A hand on my shoulder. I whip around, eyes wild. I feel like a cage animal, suddenly being released in the wild. Frantic and afraid, unsure of where to go.

The nurse's hand is firm. She meets my eyes, speaking calmly and slow. "Jack is in emergency, Cara. "

I don't question how she knows my name or that I'm family and qualify to hear client updates. Somehow she knows. Bless a small town population. "What happened?" I ask, eyes frantically searching her dark ones. "Is he okay?" I feel like I've been asking the same question over and over, never receiving a concrete answer.

The nurse looks behind me where Aunt Jill is sitting. I glance behind me, hoping an answer lies behind. That Jack will suddenly appear, saying he was just playing a joke on us. Or that he got tired of hiding and was coming to see why we weren't looking for him, that we obviously didn't know the rules of Hide and Go Seek

But all I find is my aunt, head in her hands, doubled over in pain. She's trembling, the sobs raking through her thin body, as powerful as a tornado wind against a flimsy tree.

"Will someone *please* tell me where Jack is?" I scream, wrenching myself out of the nurse's grip.

Suddenly, Uncle Randy appears, cast in place, bandage over his right eyebrow. "Cara! Relax." He grips both of my shoulders.

I rip myself free. "Where is Jack? What happened?"

He looks over top of me, at the nurse. "I'll take it from here, Wendy."

She nods sadly and leaves us to endure our pain as a family.

Uncle Randy's grip tightens and he looks me straight in the eye. I swallow back a lump in my throat, not daring to breath. "Where is Jack?" I ask wearily, suddenly exhausted, the adrenaline rush finally running dry.

"He's in surgery."

"Why?" I cling to him, feeling so small and not because of my uncle's large build or towering height. Because of a circumstance I can't control. Helpless. A failure. Like I should have been there to protect Jack from whatever monstrous thing hurt him.

Uncle Randy leads me to a seat, a few over from Aunt Jill. Likely to spare her from hearing the details all over again. "We were crossing the highway to go to McDonalds, the one across the highway from the restaurant. Jack wanted ice cream. A truck ran a red light and hit him." Uncle Randy voice is void of emotion, like he's merely repeating facts. "They tried, Cara." Sorrow dips into his voice and he hangs his head.

This time I reach out to comfort, my hand on his shoulder. "They tried what, Uncle Randy?"

After what feels like eternity, he lifts his bloodshot eyes to meet mine. "To save his legs."

His words hit me, impacting me like concrete. Cruel pictures and scenes assault me. Jack lying in a hospital bed, only half a body remaining. Jack sprawled on the payment, screaming for help. The truck driver screeching to a stop and jumping out of his truck, Uncle Randy crawling over to his son, his screams matching the decibels of Jack's.

I shudder, *I can't handle this God! Stop it, stop the images!* My throat closes, blocking air from filling my lungs. *Help me, God!* I silently cry. *I can't handle this, it's too much! I can't breathe!*

A whoosh of breeze blows over my soul, overwhelming my hysteria. Suddenly, the supernatural opens my air way. Greedily, I gulp back a breath of air. I'm still clammy all over. My forehead is slick with sweat, greasy with makeup and wet with tears, but I can breathe now.

A verse from 1 Corinthians fills my mind. Something Joey's dad preached on last Sunday. *The Bible says the Lord will never allow you to be tempted beyond what you can resist,"* Pastor Harvey had told the congregation. *"But another way to look at that verse is that the Lord will never give you more than He is strong enough to carry you through."*

Strength not of my own fills me, beginning from my toes, travelling up my torso, to my chest, and ending at the top of my head. Where determination and perseverance, resiliency and faith in a powerful and compassionate God reside.

Maybe I wasn't very helpful for my aunt when I arrived at the hospital, screaming at her for answers. But I can do a three-sixty turn now, morphing into the girl whose calming coached Aunt Jill on the drive over. And I have two hands along with my mouth.

"When you're all out of faith, I'll give you some of mine," I say, pulling Uncle Randy to his feet. I lead him over to Aunt Jill. "It's a lyric from a song by Christian artist Colton Dixon." Uncle Randy drops wearily beside his wife. She leans into him, eyes closed, face pained. I can't imagine what she must be feeling. Her little boy is alone in surgery and she's not there to hold or comfort him. Maybe not even during the moment he wakes and discovers he's missing his legs.

I stay with them throughout the night. Holding their hands. Reciting Bible verses that come to mind. Praying out loud and also silently for them. I thank God that our small hospital is equipped to do intense surgeries like amputations, due to a specialist moving here a few years ago. Uncle Randy and Aunt Jill remain quiet and when we all run out of tears, we just hold each other some more, crying out to God that the surgery will be successful.

That Jack is still Jack when it's over.

Around three in the morning, someone clears their throat behind me. I turn.

It's Joey.

I stand, my body aching from sitting in a crouch before my aunt and uncle for so long. I don't say anything. I just walk into his open arms.

"Cara, you should have called," he murmurs, holding me tight. "My dad woke me up to tell me. He assumed I was with you already." Our fight is fully forgotten and forgiven. Tragedy has that affect.

I honestly haven't even thought of it. "I guess I didn't need you." Realizing how heartless my words sound, I pull away. "Because God was here with me. I felt His presence. Giving me strength." An overwhelming thought boomerangs at me, epiphany dawning. All summer, I thought Joey was the answer to my prayer, my reason for less anxiety over my body. In reality, it was God using Joey. I wasn't been feeling Joey's hands helping me to my feet. I was experiencing the strong and supernatural hands of God, extending through another life.

Just like I was doing tonight, with my family. Being the hands of God.

Joey nods, his faith and own life experiences, in and out of the emergency room, allowing him to understand. "How are Randy and Jill?"

I look behind me. They are huddled together, having not moved once since Uncle Randy sat down. Their heads are bent together, their lips moving, eyes closed. Still praying.

I look back at Joey. "They are relying on God to carry them through."

My body aches as I wake the next morning. Sleeping sitting up in a plastic waiting room chair is hard on the body, young or not. Family members and church congregation members are scattered around the room. I'm thankful for their presence but glad for the delay. God knew our family needed to be alone last night. But the words spoken to God on our behalf through the prayer chain was definitely felt. Joey told us when he arrived that people were taking shifts praying for thirty minutes at a time, all through the night, until word was given that Joey was out of surgery and awake.

"Do you want anything from the cafeteria?" I ask Uncle Randy and Aunt Jill, stretching. Beside me, Joey is still sleeping, hair a mess. He's wearing the dress shirt from our date, rumpled now, evidence that he threw on the first thing he'd seen. Likely from a pile of clothes on his floor. I honestly wouldn't' have cared if he came in his pajamas.

"Maybe some orange juice," Uncle Randy requests. Aunt Jill shakes her head but I pick up a few oversized bran muffins and fruit salad cups anyways. Just in case she changes her mind.

Hours trickle by. Breakfast turns to noon, visitors come and go. Some bring words of encouragement or silent hands to the shoulder, symbolising prayers and extended strength to borrow.

I watch the short exchanges, God still working on my heart. *It's incredible what our bodies can do,* I think in amazement.

I tell Joey my thoughts as we walk by the nursery, stretching our legs. We stop to peer into the glass at the newborns in basinets. "It's true," he agrees. "God equipped our body with limbs, eyesight and hearing in order to help the hurting."

"Eye sight is slightly overreacted," I say.

Joey looks at me. He knows what I mean. That even blind, he's very capable of reaching to the need.

I'm the one that frowns, realizing I made a joke. Usually our relationship is marked with laughter but for the last few hours, my ears haven't heard a single joyous sound.

"It's okay to smile, even when it's raining," Joey says, quietly. "Job was a Bible character who had everything taken away from him. His family was killed, his health destroyed and possessions and work snatched from him." His arm slings around my shoulder, comforting me, making me feel like I'm not alone. "Yet he still *chose* to have joy."

"Okay," is all I say. We stay there a few more minutes and then head back to the waiting room.

A doctor is just walking up to where my aunt is talking with a church lady. She holds a plate of saran wrapped chocolate chip cookies, a gift from the other woman. She looks up, eyes fearful when she sees the doctor. On her other side, Uncle Randy reaches for her hand. A united force. Ready to meet whatever news the doctor delivers. But not as a two person team. Rather, a team of three.

God is here, no valley changes that truth. I lean into Joey for support, not sure if it's wise to be standing. "The doctor's talking to them," I tell him, too far away to overhear.

"What's he saying?" he asks, his body tensing.

"I don't know." I watch Uncle Randy and Aunt Jill hanging onto what the doctor is saying. The man nods then shows them something on his clip board. Aunt Jill asks another question and when the doctor nods, she starts sobbing, leaning into my uncle.

Uncle Randy holds her, stroking her hair. From those close enough to overhear the exchange, I know all I need to know about the conversation with the doctor. Faces are smiling, hands pointed heaven ward. It can only mean one thing: *Jack is awake.*

***

"Hey, buddy," I say, a few hours later, walking into Jack's room. He's been up for a couple hours. Aunt Jill was ushered in before Jack was fully awake and realized his legs were gone. She was able to quietly explain he'd been in an accident and what the doctors had needed to do.

Jack didn't wake up alone, to two less limbs. A mother's worst nightmare avoided.

"Hey, Cara," he says, offering a weak smile.

I sit down on the end of the bed, trying not to dwell on the lack of body bulging underneath the covers on the lower half of the bed. Uncle Randy and Aunt Jill silently leave, giving Joey and I a moment with my beloved little cousin.

Jack spots Joey standing behind me. "Hi, Joey."

"Hey, Jack." Joey seems more at ease then I am. Maybe being in Jack's position, a loss of a body part already personally experienced, makes him less worried about saying the wrong thing. "We're so glad you're okay."

Jack doesn't meet our eyes. He fingers the fur on the ear of his teddy bear that someone brought from home. "I'm okay but I don't have legs anymore."

I suck in, sharp. I have no idea how to respond.

Thankfully, Joey does. "But you're still alive, buddy." He uses the railing of the bed to guide himself to the headboard.

Stopping, he peers down at Jack. "I know exactly how you feel, Jack."

Jack looks up, his eyes pooling with tears. "But when you're blind you can still run around on the playground with friends. And go swimming. And rollerblading and..." his voice breaks and he hangs his head. "No one will want to be my friend anymore."

"Aww, Jack," I rise and stand next to Joey. "Anyone would be privileged to have you as a friend."

"But I won't be any fun. I can't do anything anymore."

Uncle Randy and Aunt Jill are back, standing quietly in the doorway listening, letting us finish our moment and conversation.

"Not true," Joey shakes his head firmly. "You know how I can still play piano, even when I can't see?"

"Yeah."

"I had to learn how to play differently after I had my accident. But I can still play."

Jack is quiet, sniffing. "But how can I use my legs differently if the doctor took them?"

Now it's my turn. "They have pretend legs you can get, Jack. Called prosthetic legs. "

He scrunches his face. "Like Terry Fox?"

Joey and I answer at the same time. "Exactly."

"Hmm. We do the Terry Fox Walk every September, to raise money for cancer research," Jack tells us, again fingering the ear of his stuffed toy. "And Terry had curly hair like mine, except red."

I hear a small gasp behind me. I look over. Silent tears are streaming down Aunt Jill's face. Thankfulness for our words spill from her eyes, in the form of her tears.

I turn my attention back to Jack. "And Terry Fox even ran with his prosthetic leg." I'm certain it was a "God thing" that Jack thought of the Canadian legion, Terry Fox. I watched a documentary on the dynamic young man who tried to run across Canada to raise money for cancer, a personal battle he was fighting himself. He didn't finish, sickness getting in the way. But people are still raising money every September, thanks to Terry's big dreams and ambitions.

Joey nods. "One of the guys I played basketball with in university, has two prosthetics legs. And Nick was one of our fastest players."

I'm surprised. Joey doesn't like to talk about basketball, let alone his years of university. Too many painful memories of a dark time in his life. Even if he is in a much better place now. I take Joey's hand and squeeze it, showing I know how hard it is for him to say that, but that the pain is worth it helping Jack.

But Jack doesn't know the pain. "Cool," he says. He notices his mom and dad. "Do you think I could try out for basketball someday, Mom?"

She comes over, a hand to her throat, trying to hold her emotions in. "For sure, honey. Anything you want to do. We can find creative ways to do it."

"Let's go," I tell Joey, leading him from the room.

Uncle Randy stops us at the door. "You two, what you just did in there..." his voices catches. I'm not used to seeing my uncle so serious, let alone crying.

He doesn't have to elaborate. "Just being the hands, feet, heart and mouth of God," I say, smiling.

He nods, his eyes saying a thanks his throat won't allow.

And as Joey and I walk outside to get some fresh air and some sleep, hand in hand into the sunlight, I know exactly what God is doing right now. Smiling down at us from heaven, rejoicing because I've finally got it. Finally realized what my body is:

A tool to love.

Chapter 8

Two weeks later, I find myself staring at an empty pulpit on the stage. The worship team, sermon, and visiting congregation afterwards are long gone. Lunch dates and Sunday afternoon plans have been made, the main entrance visiting area now quiet. My gaze settles on the wooden cross hanging on the wall. I think of God and all He's teaching me through the trial my family is traveling through.

Persevering through on faith alone.

My head rests on Joey's shoulder. We've been sitting here for what feels like hours. Though I'm sure the church service has only been over for a little while.

"What are you thinking about?" Joey asks, brushing a stray curl aside, kissing my forehead.

I sigh. "Jack." Always Jack. The house feels eerily empty this week. Uncle Randy, Aunt Jill and Jack are all in Toronto. They plan to stay for the remainder of August, possibly more. As long as it takes for Jack to become comfortable with being an amputee and using his new legs. They were referred to the special children's program for recent amputees there. The brochure Aunt Jill showed me describes a child friendly way of teaching how to live with a loss of a limb, how to care for prosthetics and the possibilities still available even after an accident.

My legs are curled up underneath me. Grey yoga pants, a dark navy long sleeve, curls spiraling out of control and a makeup free face is my look today. Comfort is my friend these days.

"Joey?"

He looks down. "Yeah?"

"I changed my mind."

"About what?"

I sit up, sitting cross legged now. "About being the guest speaker for camp."

His face lights up and his posture straightens. "Really?" Excitement fills his voice. "What changed your mind?"

"I think that God doesn't give us our victory stories to remain silent. They are meant to share." And my lessons on how to change my view on my body and disabilities, like Jack and Joey's, could be life changing for some of the teens that week. "I have just one condition."

"What?"

"You follow up my speaking with a song." He listens as I describe the song I have in mind. It's a song by Francesca Battiselli called "Hands of God". Throughout the song, the artist sings about people in her life whose words and actions make her feel God's love and presence. To her, these people are the hands of God Himself, reaching out to support her. Through saying the words she needs to hear, stopping what they are doing to help her, or offering a hand to the shoulder when she's hurting.

Joey nods when I finish my explanation. Remembering I have my phone with me, I reach for my brown messenger bag and pull my phone out along with a pair of white headphones.

"Here," I hand him one part of my earphones, placing the other in my own ear. "Listen to the song. I have it on my phone."

He puts the earphone in and we lean our faces close, to keep the headphones in place. As the song begins, Joey closes his eyes, the words washing over him. Francesca Battiselli has a wonderful soulful sound but I can't wait to hear how Joey's God given talent will sound singing the powerful lyrics. I don't have to ask if he can learn the chords and lyrics in time for the camp next week.

By the time the chorus comes around for third time, Joey sings along. His voice makes me tremble. It's like a glimpse of the angels above, their choir a melody beyond the ability of most humans. The song finishes and Joey pulls his earphone out. "I've never heard that song before."

I take the earphone. "So will you do it?"

"Definitely."

Six days later, I'm back in the auditorium, this time standing off to the side of the stage. A group of thirty-five teens fill the pews before me. Trying to steady my nerves and shaking hands, I take a deep breath. Unlike during school oral presentations, I feel like my lunch will stay down. God is giving me supernatural courage and ability.

Joey has a look on his face at the piano, one I've come to associate with praying. No doubt he's sending up prayers on my behalf. For calm of nerves and confidence, to listen to God's leading for words and for prepared hearts to accept what I'm about to share.

After David introduces me, I step to the center of the stage and wave. "Hey, guys. Like David said, I have a personal story that really ties into your camp theme of loving yourself."

Once I begin, girls straighten in their seats and boys look up in interest. Though I don't share all the details, I remain appropriately transparent. Through sharing my struggles with an eating disorder and then living in a healthy sized body, I see something in their eyes and expressions.

Identification with living with hurt, flaws, insecurity and silent pain.

Though I'm not sure what lies they are believing in their heads, I know when I labour for the Lord it's never in vain. 1 Corinthians 15:58 says so and I believe it with my entire heart.

I shuffle my typed papers, suddenly feeling a sense to stray from my notes. I already explained about my past and my struggles of the summer when I viewed myself as heavier and not healthier. "But God taught me a lot this summer about loving myself." I set the papers down and walk to the side of the pulpit. "He taught me that as a human, my need for belonging and acceptance will never change." I know this all by heart now. "But what *can* change is how I view myself."

I see a girl in the front, who looks unnaturally thin, hanging onto my story and words. It's as if I can hear her heart's cry asking, *How do I change the warped way I see myself?*

To her silent cry, I sum up my God given epiphany of three weeks earlier in the waiting room. "God allowed me to change my view of myself this summer by helping me see my body as individual parts, capable of encouraging people by using the gift of my arms, legs and mouth. And when I started using that perspective when I thought of my body, things changed. The lies in my head and comparisons started to fade. And they don't stick around as long when they do invite themselves into my mind now. My new way of thinking about myself makes them feel unwelcome."

I walk over to the grand piano. Joey's already there, fingers hovering over the keys. "You're on," I whisper. "Go get 'em for God. Use that beautiful gift of a voice to be His hands."

"Always, Cara, always."

I find a seat in the front pew, next to the thin girl I noticed before. Together, we listen to Joey's rendition of Francesca's song "Hands of God." Snapshots from the summer wash over me as I listen. It's as if God is giving me a glimpse of times where He crossed my path with people, where they were the hands of God to me. But I also see instances where I was used as well. I flash back to the waiting room with Uncle Randy and Aunt Jill. Then to the hospital room with Jack, talking about Terry Fox.

God, You are so good, even in the storm. Beauty from ashes is truly an attribute of Yours.

When the last note is played, I realize I'm crying. "It moved me too," the girl tells me, wiping at her eyes, staring at the piano.

I look at her and then without an invitation, pull her into a hug. Though I don't know her name or story, I can sense the hurt.

God uses me that day. To speak life to a handful of teens who come up to me afterwards, opening up to me about their own distorted views of themselves. Worthless and deserving cutting. Unlovable because of past mistakes. Some are like I was, striving to reach and maintain unrealistic and unhealthy goals for themselves.

When the last teen has left for the day, I feel drained. But happy. Today God used me in big ways. "I'm sure your story helped others who didn't come up afterwards to talk or thank you," Mandy tells me, placing her guitar back in the case.

I continue winding a blue extension cord up. "Good point."

David calls her over to help him find something.

I finish winding the cord and set it next to the pile I already finished. Then I join Joey by the piano. He's quietly playing the music for "Hands of God." I wish he was singing but before I can ask him to, he stops playing. "I have something for you." He fishes around in the pocket of his green and grey plaid shirt. Out comes a folded white piece of paper. He hands it to me. "It's words that came to me the first day we met, after we went for our walk. It never seemed like the right time to give it to you." He watches me unfold the paper. "But last night I got a feeling today would include a moment that felt right. This feels like that moment."

I'm not sure if it's a poem or lyrics, what's scribbled in pencil, but it's obviously in Joey's handwriting. Whatever it is, the words are stunning. Like words penned by God Himself.

But aren't you beautiful?

In the eyes of the One who matters most?

Yes, in His eyes you're past pretty,

Far more stunning then the stars.

Yes, from His lips comes three words,

That He uses to describe you:

Breathtaking beyond belief.

I let the powerful words wash over me. I read them twice. Then again. Once more. "Joey," I look up, reaching out to touch his face. His face is rough, slight growth of a beard evident. The ruggedly handsome version of him. "Thank you. Reading these is like hearing God's voice through yours."

"The theme of our summer, it seems."

"I couldn't agree more." I know I'll treasure these words forever. And maybe someday they will help other woman and men, to see themselves as God does.

I gaze up into the vivid ocean blue eyes of a man I adore beyond words. I can't wait to experience more of life with him, more opportunities to be extensions of God to the world together.

"Let's be a force to be reckoned with," I tell him, brushing his dark brown hair off his forehead. "A power couple for expanding the Kingdom of Christ."

He kisses me in agreement.

After that, his hands return to the keys and he begins to sing "Hands of God" once more. I join in quietly, growing in passion as the song proceeds. We've never sang together before but our voices sound pleasant together. I usually don't sing loud in public, worried about how I compare to others. But after the lessons of this summer? I'm exposing that fear with the voice of God, someone who hears voices singing praise to Him as they truly are, when sung from the heart:

Angelic.

***

Joey hands me a pink rose. It's my favourite kind, from his mom's stunning garden.

Today's my last day in town. By this time tomorrow, I'll be moving back in with roommates, unpacking and getting ready for another university year.

"These are the best," I say, breathing in deeply.

"I've been dreading this day," Joey confesses quietly.

I sit down on the front step. Familiar territory for a heart to heart. "We did a good job of avoiding it all summer."

"Yeah, not sure if that was wise."

"Worrying about it would've just stolen the joy from our current days."

"True." He gazes out, not seeing the striking red and orange sunset that I do.

I describe it to him and he seems distracted, not as interested as usual in hearing my descriptions of scenery. I try to engage him in conversation, memories and funny moments from the summer but nothing works.

I can't put my finger on it. He seems understandably sad but something else. It takes a moment of studying him before I identify it.

Why does he look nervous? If I were a gambling girl, I'd say he looks identical to the way he did before he asked me at the campfire to be his official girlfriend.

"This isn't right." He says, standing abruptly. He pulls me up beside him. "I thought it was, but it's not."

He leads me by the hand back inside. The house is empty, his family is camping at the Saskatchewan Landing for the weekend. I follow behind him, confused. We end up at the piano. He sits down and I continue to stand. He doesn't look at me but takes a deep breath, as if to prepare for a well-rehearsed speech. "Cara, I need to play you something." Without waiting, he launches into a song myself and the world know well, Bruno Mars "Just the Way You Are."

I sit down next to him, the rose on my lap. His voice is pure and passionate. The loveliest sound I've ever experienced in a singer. Soft, yet strong. Unique, but now familiar to me.

Halfway through the song, he stops. "That doesn't feel right either." His hands drop to his side.

"Joey, what's going on?" I'm so confused. The song was going flawlessly. *Why did he stop?*

"It just doesn't seem right," he mutters to himself. Then, as if a light bulb flashes in his mind, his hands return to the piano keys. A soft intro of chords begins, intricate but simple to describe as heavenly. Next, the words come. I recognize them immediately. I see them every day, taped to my bathroom mirror.

"But aren't you beautiful? In the eyes of the One who matters most?" Joey's fingers dance over the keys, creating a divine sound. "More stunning the stars?" He continues to bring to life the words he shared with me the last day of camp.

I'm captivated, in a trance and in awe. Somehow I know this is new, not something rehearsed. God is giving Joey the right chords and melody to match the words as he plays. In this moment, I fall in love all over with God. And with this wonderful and caring man He's given to me.

When he finishes, Joey turns to meet my eyes. "Cara, God is the One who matters most, the One who describes you as breathtaking beyond belief."

I gasp as he slides off the piano bench and onto one knee. He reaches into his pocket. "And I want to be the man to remind you of that fact for the rest of your days." He opens the black box, revealing a glittering silver ring. "So what do you say? Can I have forever with you?"

Tears sliding down my face, I slip to the ground beside him. "Forever sounds wonderful," I whisper then fling myself into his arms.

Eventually, we part, both our eyes shining. Joey slips the ring on my finger and I raise it to the light, admiring it. "You really surprised me." I wasn't expecting this but it feels so right now that the moment had arrived.

"So did you. I wasn't expecting to meet someone like you this summer."

"You and me both," I say, leaning into my fiancés' arms. He wraps me into a tight hug and we remain that way into the early hours of the next morning, dreaming and believing in the hope of tomorrow. All because we both serve a loving God who adores to surprise His creations.

With wonderful crossed paths.

Epilogue

Our engagement is a long one, two years. This allows me to finish up my education degree, find a job at Westberry Elementary School as a grade one teacher, for Joey to finish seminary and take over his dad's retirement from lead pastor and for us to save for a down payment on a small house. We plan to stay in Kindersley. The house we have our eye on is right across the street from the church.

The years between the wedding and the proposal were long yet swift. Like Uncle Randy told me, long distance relationships are rough. But we managed, visiting each other on weekends, phoning and even sending handwritten letters in the mail. A few times, we'd watch the same movie in our different locations, while talking on the phone. A fun way to have a date night when far away. Skype dates over the supper hour were common too, a mock dinner date, even if I was having cereal for supper and he was eating spaghetti. Sort of like going to a restaurant, I suppose. You don't always order the same thing as your date. Each summer, I returned to Kindersley, working at the restaurant one summer and as a lifeguard at the pool another summer.

"I can't believe you're getting married," Aunt Jill gushes, teary eyed. She and my mom are helping me get ready in the upstairs room. Sunlight streams through the open window, a refreshing breeze filtering through. The perfect kind of day for a backyard wedding at Joey's parents.

"It feels like a dream," I admit, studying myself in the antique floor length mirror in the Waterloo's guestroom. "But we're more than ready to take this next step. I can't wait to exchange my title of fiancée to wife."

My mom fusses with the hem of my dress as Aunt Jill tucks an orange tiger lily flower behind my ear. My curls are completely natural today. Wild and free. Curling up a beautiful storm. They're longer then I've worn them in a while, laying just past my shoulders.

A knock on the door.

Aunt Jill opens it, revealing Uncle Randy. "Are you ready for her?" Aunt Jill asks.

Uncle Randy nods, taking in the sight of me in my wedding dress. "Yes, especially the one at the end of the aisle. He's bouncing with excitement." I lift my dress so I don't trip and move to the doorway. He kisses me on the check. "You look radiant, Cara. Absolutely stunning."

"Thanks." A pang of sadness fills me. I wish Joey could see me walking down the aisle towards him. But that's not fruitful thinking, so I push the thought aside. Today is a day to celebrate what I do have. *Who* I have in my life.

"Ready?" My mom asks.

I take a deep breath. "I want to get this all over with, so yes!"

"Nerves are normal," my mom and Aunt Jill say in unison. We all laugh and it lessens the nervous feeling.

They help me down the stairs, helping me hold in the puffy crinoline underneath my Cinderella wedding dress. The plan is for Aunt Jill and my mom to open the French doors leading to the patio. Then I'll exit, walking down the patio steps to the grass path, between the set up white chairs on either side of the path.

My bridesmaids are waiting at the French doors. They both "Ooh" and "Ahh" when they see me approach.

"Cara," Mandy rushes over. "If you take *my* breath away, imagine what you're going to do to Joey!"

Another pang. He won't be able to see me. Again, I try to bury the bitter thought. He will be able to sense the love shining in my eyes and feel the excitant in the shaking of my hands. "I'm really regretting what we did last night though."

Curious eyes pin me with questions.

Realizing what they think I'm referring to, I wave my hands. "No! Not that. We haven't... we waited..."

Mandy smooths the front of her strapless, knee length baby blue dress. She wears a white tiger lily behind her ear. Her once trademark blond dreadlocks were cut out last year. Her new, short, pixie haircut matches her spunky personality perfectly. Mandy doesn't know it, but David confided in Joey that tonight he's going to propose to her under the stars, when he walks her home after the reception. "Maybe you better explain yourself, Cara," Mandy says, placing one hand on her hip. "Your stumbling is not so helpful to your reputation, girl."

I take the bouquet of white roses my mom hands me. All the bridal party have identical flowers, with baby's breath and pretty green vines interspersed. All the flowers are from Joey's mom's garden. The boys wear white dress shirts, minus the suit jacket, black skinny ties and black stylish suspenders. "All I meant to say is I'm wishing Joey hadn't talked me into watching "Wedding's Gone Wrong" YouTube videos after the dress rehearsal."

The wedding party laughs. "Sounds like Joey to me," Erica shakes her head. A year and a week ago she and Isaac were married. A basketball sized round belly shows very obviously in her fitted bridesmaid dress. But she looks radiant. When they say expectant mothers glow, they weren't kidding. Today Erica's natural dark ringlets are completely down, trailing to her waist, just like the first summer we met.

"Seeing brides fall into ponds, trip down the aisle or knock the pastor out when they trip has me a little worried!" I'm being honest but the smiles of the loved ones around me help ease the fears.

Uncle Randy peers outside. "Oh! There it is. Pastor Harvey gave me the nod." The curtain falls back into place.

I bite my lip, trying not to smudge my red lipstick. No more silliness. No more dreaming or planning. *This moment is here. The one that I've thought about forever but never actually thought would arrive.*

I pinch myself, just to be sure. Mandy catches me. "Not a dream, Cara. This is your life." She smiles her encouragement and moves to her place behind Erica, the first in line since we don't have a flower girl.

When the French doors open, the pianist begins to play a pretty jazz piece entitled "Misty." There are words to it, speaking of being so misty eyed that you can't help falling in love. But today the pianist is playing the instrumental version. It's the same song my mom walked down the aisle to. Ironically, it was the same one Joey's mother walked down to. When we made the discovery during wedding planning late one night, Joey and I both agreed a third wedding was definitely in order to have the song played at. A new family tradition to be passed on.

I watch Erica slowly walk down the aisle. Then it's Mandy turn. They seem to walk too fast and yet everything seems in slow motion.

My dad takes my arm. "You're as lovely as your mother on our wedding day, Cara."

I return his smile and then step out into the sunshine.

At first my eyes take in those standing from their white folding seats. Friends, summer job co-workers, people from the church congregation, family, old roommates, sporting teammates, elementary school friends, friends of Joey, friends of mine, mutual friends...

Our walk slows when I look to the front, to those standing by the gazebo. The bridesmaids are to the left of Joey's dad, who's officiating. David, the best man, stands next to Jack. My little cousin isn't so little any more. Eleven years old and he's already taller than me. Tall and stretched out, his face has lost its slight chubbiness. A basketball player's build is in the making, something he's excited about to try out for in middle school come the start of school in September. In just two weeks from this August long weekend wedding. Jack looks so grown up standing next to the others in his wedding attire. No one would even notice the slightly uneven rhythm when he moves if you didn't tell them. His three weeks of learning how to live with prosthetic legs were invaluable. I thank God every day that the accident didn't steal my loveable cousin from our family. It definitely matured him but his smile, ever present funny comments and zest for life are still there.

Finally, after I've avoided it, I find the person I want to see the most today.

Joey. The groom. My soon to be forever husband.

It's like he senses that I'm looking at him because his face suddenly lights up like fireworks in the night sky. Even if you offered me millions, I couldn't stop my silly smile of a woman head over heels in love.

He looks every inch the prince charming I know him to be. The knight in shining armor that swept me from my feet two summers ago. *And oh, does his longer, wavy hair look handsome.* He's dressed identical to his groomsmen yet he stands out to me. Maybe it's his grown out hair, delightfully curly when it's longer. Or his fuller look from a newfound love of rowing. *No, it's not any of those.* My smile stretches even bigger. It's the childlike excitement on his face that sets him apart. The look of longing and love that comes clearer with every step I take towards him.

When we reach the others at the end of the aisle, my dad kisses the top of my head. "Love you, sweetie."

"Love you too," I whisper, already feeling the tears threating to fall.

Dad smiles then joins my mom, seated next to Joey's mom, Uncle Randy and Aunt Jill in the front row.

I turn and take the hands Joey is holding out. He leans down, his voice meant for my ears alone. "Beautiful doesn't do you justice, Cara." The sound of water falling, from the fountain nearby, fills the moment with a magical quality.

Feeling shy in front of the others and for some reason Joey, I duck my head, the start of a blush creeping in. In this gown, I feel like I could be wearing glass slippers and going to a ball. Strapless and full waisted, thanks to layers of crinoline, my reflection reminded me of Cinderella. Except my dress has a thin glittering black empire waist and sweetheart neckline. But I guess my shoes, hidden beneath my poofy dress *are* similar to

Cinderella's. Mine aren't glass but they are black, covered in glitter that matches the small wrap around section on my waist.

Joey lifts my chin with one figure, as if forgetting it's not just us. It's easier for him to forget the others when he can't see them. He leans down, about to try to convince me he's telling the truth when his dad clears his throat. "A little ahead of ourselves, aren't we, son? I believe that part comes a little later in the ceremony."

An embarrassed look. "Oh, yeah, right." He grins. "Please, proceed."

Loving the exchange, our guests chuckle and exchange happy whispers.

We're lost in each other's presence but I vaguely still hear Pastor Harvey describe our relationship as an unending triangle because we have God in the center, a shared value and large part of our individual lives. "Unlike a two point line, with end points, Joey and Cara have dedicated to include a third point into their marriage. To allow them to love beyond human abilities, borrowing a supernatural love to shower each other with. The kind of love spoken about in the thirteenth chapter of 1 Corinthians."

As his dad reads over the chapter, my eyes lock on Joey's. He hasn't stopped smiling since he took my hand. "I love you," he mouths.

I squeeze his hand, my signal that I echo the same feeling.

Before I know it, Mac is happily trotting down aisle, carrying a wicker basket with white rose petals inside. He stops at Pastor Harvey's side, dropping the basket at his feet. Mac's tongue hangs out of the side of his mouth and his golden bushy tail thumps against the grass.

Joey's dad pets Mac then lifts the basket, taking the black ring box out.

The rest of the ceremony is a blur. We say our vows, choosing traditional "To have and to hold" ones over personal ones. The exchanging of rings comes and goes and then the best part...

"Now with the power vested in me, I take it as a great privilege to announce to you, for the very first time, Mr. and Mrs. Joey Waterloo!" Joey's dad nudges his son. "Now you get to kiss the girl."

And he does. Dipping me down, Joey presses his lips down on mine. It's a passionate and deep kiss, one that earns us whistles and hoots from the guests.

Heat rushes to my cheeks when he pulls me back up. But I don't care. I'm a married woman now!

And just like that, our next adventure begins. The guests cheer, blowing bubbles on as we walk down the aisle to the pianist singing and playing Stevie Wonder's "Signed, Sealed, Delivered I'm Your's" upbeat jazz number. I loop my arm through my husband's and wave as we walk, blowing kisses to some of my younger cousins, laughing with joy when they do the same back.

A reception is planned for later that evening, after bridal party pictures around our favorite walking trail. The evening will be made up of dancing under twinkling lights, a catered dinner, various speeches, fun newlywed games and silverware tinkling against glass to encourage us to kiss.

But for now, that all feels forever away. With Joey's arm in mine, surrounded by loved ones, the sun shining down on us, I feel the overwhelming sense that God is with us, celebrating with us. Though He loves us as much as before, I'm sure He's overjoyed at the people we have become and lessons we have learned together. Overjoyed because we realized from meeting each other what we really are: An extension of the loving arms of Christ.

And love is what we fully plan to do to this world. I grip my husband's arm tighter, loving the fresh feel of being married, wondering how it can be only a few minutes old. *Because that's what this body was made to do.*

Love.

***

"Come here," Joey says once the limo door closes, giving us privacy. It's parked in the driveway of his parent's. Tin cans are attached by strings dangling from the back, the "Just Married" sign attached to the bumper. From outside the tinted windows, I hear our family and friends still cheering, waiting to wave us away for a few hours, before pictures and the reception.

For a second, I'm brought back to our first official date, the one that ended not quite as envisioned. I'm confident this limo ride won't end as abruptly. Rather, in a happily ever after kind of way. Yes, an adventure is awaiting us together, beginning the second the rings were in place, our "I do's" were said, and forever was promised to one another.

I don't need to be asked twice. I lean into him, making it easy for him to find my face. He cups my cheek and brings his lips to mine, moving them slowly in the familiar way. Passion untamed is ours now. No longer will I have to pull away from it. No, everything I have is now my husband's to have.

"Last night I had a dream," Joey says when we pull apart. His eyes are bright with excitement over the upcoming adventures and full of a love I feel reflecting back in my eyes.

"I hope it wasn't a nightmare," I laugh, reaching for the sparkling cider nestled in a bucket of ice.

"No, more like a dream literally come true."

I look up from trying to unscrew the tight lid. Whatever he's about to share, I have a feeling I won't soon forget. "What happened?"

He reaches across the seat to find my hand. When he finds it, he runs his thumb tenderly over my ring. His blue eyes are focused on my eyes, in a way they sometimes are. The ever brilliant blue of his eyes seem to search mine, finding the hallways of my heart that only he has ever seen. "It was actually a dream I'd had back in grade twelve, but it was different this year."

I hold my breath, captivated by the look in his eyes.

He runs a hand through his messy hair. I love the look, so different from when we first met. Upon my request, he'd let his hair grow out for the wedding. Ever since spotting his baby photos where he had a head of dark curls and later seeing his graduation photos with grown out hair, I was sold. When it's short, it lays flat but grown slightly longer, it curls into handsome messy waves. I'm certain our children will have wild curls. It thrills me to picture myself running my fingers through a child's hair, tucking them into bed.

"In the initial dream, I dreamt I was at my wedding, standing in these clothes, holding my wife's hands. All I could see was the back of her head." He shakes his head. "I guess I was watching the ceremony from a third person view, since I could see myself."

I'm not sure if I want to ask, but I do. "What happened in the second dream?"

His smile is slow but sure. "It was the same thing but this time I saw my bride turn around."

"And?"

"She had the same long blond wild curls as the first dream, so I knew it was the same girl I'd seen all those years ago. I didn't make the connection at first, since usually you said your hair was chin length." He reaches out, finding a long curl to twirl around his index finger.

Warmth spreads through my chest, already knowing what he's going to say next. "So you're saying you think it was me? Even in the first dream?"

Joey brings my hand to his lips and kisses it, eyes closing. Then he looks back up at me, eyes still focused on me. A wedding gift from God for the intimate moment. "I know it was, even though I've never laid eyes on you. At least not on this side of heaven. I just have this certain sense, the same sense I get when someone needs praying for, that it was you and how you look today. "

I giggle as he kisses my cheek, tickling my skin. "How can you be sure, aside from the coincidence of the blond curls? Lots of girls have long, curly blond hair."

His leans in, whispering in my ear. "Because God wanted me to know how you looked, so I could tell you something in this moment."

My breath catches, again certain I will remember his words until the day I die. "What?"

"That even though you are the most elegant bride I've ever seen, the woman I've fallen in love with is even more stunning."

My voice is a whisper, like his. "What girl was that?"

He whispers his answer, just before brushing his lips against mine. "The girl inside."

***

I prop myself up on one elbow and take in the beautiful soul lying on the bed beside me, half covered in white sheets.

Joey Waterloo, a gift from God. I have no doubt in my mind that God places people in our lives, just when we need them. To learn from their experiences and be changed through their talents and unique personalities. To be strengthened through their prayers.

I watch the slow rise and fall of my new husband's chest. Even in his sleep, he wears a smile. One hand rests behind his head the other lying across his bare chest. I no longer have to wonder what he looks like first thing in the morning. Mused brown hair, slight rugged stubble on his chin and soft breathing are a lovely sight. Worth the wait.

I look down at the simple silver band Joey placed on my finger, not twenty four hours ago. Beautiful. Just like this relationship. Just like me. The way I am today.

"Good morning, wife," Joey says, eyes slowly opening, sleepy smile turning to a grin.

I learn down and kiss him softly. "Hello, husband."

We spend the entire morning cuddling in bed, dreaming of tomorrows and reminiscing about yesterdays. The first summer we met, the ones in between and the reception the night before. As I lay in my husband's arms, safe and sound, I can't help but happily sigh.

I'm so thankful for that summer we met. God used Joey to make me realize what my body is capable of. With my warped self-perception blocking my view, I hadn't been seeing it for what it was. A tool to change the world.

Again, I look to my hand, noticing not the ring but my fingers. I turn them over, marvelling at what they can accomplish. All along I've had hands to help someone up and arms to reach out to hug the hurting.

I feel Joey's heart beating behind me as I lean into him. *I have a heart to be filled with compassion for a person in need.*

My eyes travel to my legs, covered by the sheets. *And I have two legs that allow me to walk and talk with others, to encourage them with my mind, full of personal experiences and wisdom learned from those experiences.*

I picture our first kiss as man and wife and the sweet private kisses of the night before. *And I have the ability to speak life through the words I say. To build up the torn down and lonely lives all around.*

Yes, this body is capable of so much. And from this day forward, I refuse to belittle it. I *choose* to see it for what it really is, the way God and Joey have seen it all along. As a resource to change the world. Lift others up.

And that makes it a beautiful body.

As sleep sets in, I snuggle deeper into the most wonderful man I know. His arms around me are more muscular then our first summer together. He's not the lanky young adult he was back then but an older man, more filled out but still fit. I don't mind the extra muscle one bit. More strength to secure me and hold me close with.

Feelings of happiness flood throughout my entire being, surging through my veins and overflowing my spirit. After years of battling the image in the mirror, of comparing and never measuring up, I'm finally done. Relief has finally come. Followed by freedom. And lasting change. Yes, bad body image days will likely still come. But now, I'll strive to remember my new definition of beauty, not based on the physical but on the *capabilities* of the physical. Happy sigh.

Finally, beauty redefined.

Acknowledgements:

As always, all glory and ultimate thanks first goes to **my precious Jesus**, my forever best friend. There wouldn't even be an acknowledgement page without the words You gave me for this powerful love story. Father, I'll be honest, I didn't want to write this book. After a two year hiatus from writing, I was very resistant when You gave me the idea for *Blinded*. Even if it was actually an answer to a prayer I'd requested. I'd been listening to Colbie Caillat's song "Try" and was overwhelmed with the world's need to redefine their narrow definition of beauty.

"God, use me to do this," I pleaded as I walked that August afternoon in my hometown of Kindersley, Saskatchewan. Suddenly, a name came to mind.

"Oh, no, not again," I thought, knowing the significance of that. You see, whenever I have written a novel before, the first thing that comes to mind is usually the main character's name, followed by the moral of the story and then the title. Some authors choose those last. But once I have those in mind, the story just flows.

"Not doing it," I told God. "But I am curious about this name. What is Joey Waterloo like?"

"You'll have to write the story, if you want to find out," I heard God chuckle across my heart.

Since you've just finished reading this story, you know I finally surrendered and wrote the book. It was the fastest book I've ever written. In just nine days, amongst work and friends,

God flowed a story through my fingertips. I had been praying for more healing, summer 2014. I was thinking God could bring more friends or wise mentors my way, like real people, but He used my brief week with these amazing characters to speak truth and healing into my life.

Like Cara, I had an eating disorder in high school. And like Cara, some days I still struggle with my new healthy shape. As a teenager, I quickly lost over forty pounds. I did this through intentionally starving myself to be thin. Eating was something I could control, but it soon controlled and consumed me. I was miserable, even when the scale hit the lowest weight ever of ninety-four pounds.

I also developed an addiction to exercise. It became my drug, my obsession. I gave up dreams, family time, even school, in order to reach my "exercise high." I'd exercise five hours a day, rewind the hard parts on workout DVDs and regularly push myself to physical and emotional exhaustion.

Telling my mom I had an eating disorder and that I needed help, was one of the hardest things I've ever done. But I got my life back because of it. Through my sessions at Christian Counselling Services in Saskatoon, I learned techniques to heal. I still struggle some days with body image, but I am healed. I now eat and exercise in healthy amounts. God used CCS to free me from my chains. And God can use them to heal you. Ask for help, you won't regret it. Asking for help is not a sign of weakness but strength.

If you search "Nyla Ditson" on YouTube, my testimony will come up. "Nyla Ditson Testimony April 2014" is a fifteen minute video outlining how I was finally freed from my chains (the song "What's Left of Me" that Joey sings is also on my YouTube channel!). God didn't intend for us to live chained and wants to help. Take the first step to ask for help and you'll start to see things change. You'll still have tough and insecure days, but you'll be free.

So God? Thank You for giving me the idea for this book. For giving me another beauty from ashes moment. Thank You for using a terrible thing like addiction and disorder and using it to help others in the end.

Secondly, I would like to thank my counsellor, **Heather Tomes**. When I decided I needed help, I looked up Christian Counselling Services in my area. When CCS's website came up, I scrolled through the photos of the counsellors. Seeing a smiling, kind looking, young and blond woman, I decided to book an appointment with her. Over the course of a few years, God used Heather to free me from my chains. She taught me how to change my thinking about my body, how to set up guardrails, and how to write truth statements on recipe cards. One card I still read regularly is "Nyla, your worth is not defined by what you eat or how much you exercise. Rest feels good! Don't forget that! Your identity is found in being a friend of Christ, something that won't ever change from day to day." Check out my testimony on YouTube for more of the practical tips Heather taught me.

Heather, you were a Godsend. In that dark time of my life, your office was a safe haven. I felt protected there. And so cared for. God gave you such insight and wisdom into my situation. I wouldn't be where I am today, functioning at work and school, living a balanced life of work and rest, dreaming of love, enjoying hobbies and family or as in love with Jesus as I am, if it weren't for you. Because of your help, I have my life back. I can experience that full life God intends for all of us. Keep speaking life and truth into your client's life. Words can't express what it means to them. I will be forever grateful for you and how you invested into me.

Thirdly, **Heidi Huizing**. Thank you for sharing the lyrics of "What's Left of Me." I was honored to be loaned them and trusted enough to give them a melody and music. How special is it that we wrote a song together? Next time I sing it at church, I want you there, singing harmony with me. The characters of Joey and Cara are a mix of both our personalities. Lessons you taught me are now forever in fiction within this book, for the world to learn. Our friendship is one that will withstand the test of time and living in different provinces. Thank you for being my "Joey" and being obedient to pray for me that day, when the driver I was with fell asleep at the wheel. God heard your prayers for my safety, even if you didn't know at the time why I was in danger. Thank you for your friendship, girl! You mean the world to me! Although, I am a bit afraid what kind of stories you will tell at open mike time during my future wedding! Please, be kind :)

Fourthly, to the **staff at Simply Elevate Magazine**. You have all been so supportive and helpful in advertising my personal ministry of writing. I recently read a powerful article by David Platt. He used the image of the Amazon River, symbolizing the potential power for telling others about God and strengthening friendships with God already in place, *when we join together*. Single drops of melted ice water from the Andes Mountains fall to the Amazon. Each drop by itself is small, but together they create the mightiest river on earth. Platt writes. "Flowing into the Atlantic Ocean at a rate of more than seven million cubic feet per second, the Amazon is more powerful then the next ten largest rivers in the world *combined!*" I have been praying for people to be an "Amazon Army" with me for God. I came into contact with you all, through a God orchestrated event with Sally Meadows at my work. She was the one to introduce me to you. Now I'm writing for an amazing Christian magazine alongside you! Thank you for your hearts for Jesus. Thank you for letting me be a part of your powerful team. Thank you for being encouragers and role models to this baby of the Simply Elevate team!

Fifthly, to **Kelli Snider**. Thank you, friend, for editing *Blinded.* You gave such good advice, from grammar corrections to content changes. I especially loved the side notes you scribbled in the corner of the pages, sharing what parts spoke to you the most. As a writer, it means so much to hear specific parts that helped people. As I wrote *Blinded,* I prayed that God would give me specific wording that future readers would personally connect to. Your comments proved that God was listening, as always, loud and clear!

And sixthly, again to **Jesus**. This story is Yours alone. Take it to the world, Jesus. Not to just a small stage, but to the nations. So many men and woman need to learn to see themselves differently. As powerful beings with body parts to change the world. Use this book to free the chained and to help the world realize that beauty and feelings fade, but love remains, something we should focus on. I love You, Lord. You are so good. Always providing and surprising me. Keep using me and this book in big and unexpectant ways, to draw people to You and to heal wounds. And thank You, for making me realize that I have arms to hug, ears to listen, a mouth to encourage and legs to walk alongside the hurting. My body parts are powerful. Help the world and I to remember this and to use our limbs to change the world, to love the world to You.